The Pragmatist's Guide to Life

A Guide to Creating Your Own Answers to Life's Biggest Questions

By Simone & Malcolm Collins

http://Pragmatist.Guide

Read this Book with a Friend

The manner in which our brains process the information we read is different from the manner in which they process information during a social interaction. Discussing each chapter with someone you trust will allow you to more thoughtfully consider life's big questions and build yourself into the type of person you ultimately decide you want to be.

At your request, we will provide your desired reading companion with a free digital copy of this book: http://pragmatist.guide/bookbuddy/

Get a Free Audiobook

Should you prefer listening to books over reading them, visit: http://pragmatist.guide/audiobook/ to request an audiobook and we'll send one to you for free. (We offer free audiobooks for all the books we write.)

Table of Contents

About This Guide

As humans, we get to choose what we believe and who we want to be. These are the most important decisions we will ever make.

The vast majority of people never exercise their freedom to choose their identity and beliefs. Instead, they allow others to tell them who they are, choosing only a few trivial differentiating traits for themselves. When they react angrily or generously, they ascribe the personality that led them to that behavior as being something outside their control. This is because in their minds "who they are" is something outside of their control.

We live life as a sticky ball rolling down a sidewalk, picking up a hodgepodge of stuff that just happens to be in our path. It is natural to try to convince ourselves that this hodgepodge is "who we really are." We tell ourselves this lie because thinking is hard, and society doesn't give us a good framework for structuring our beliefs about ourselves and the world. Instead, we are served a smorgasbord of prefabricated worldviews and told we have the option to choose among them.

Worse, we live in a society in which there is no profession or organization we can turn to for help answering life's big questions that will not pressure us to adopt beliefs closer to their own. If you ask them what you should want to do with your life, they tell you to do "good" things and then explain to you what you should believe "good" is. This is not due to any flaw in these individuals or institutions, but the fact that these institutions are designed from the ground up to lead people to the answers they believe are right. There is no institution, framework, or guide designed from the ground up to help people come up with their own conclusions.

The Pragmatist's Guide to Life was written to remedy this. The book lays out the applied pragmatic thought framework for systematically constructing one's own beliefs about the world, leveraging those beliefs to decide who to be as a person, and creating the person one wants to be.

The Pragmatist's Guide to Life is a product of the Pragmatist Foundation, a nonprofit dedicated to pragmatically yet audaciously tackling life's biggest questions and challenges. Since this book was first published, additional books in the series on relationships, sexuality, and governance structures have been released. Currently we are working on building a K-12 school system. All our projects are a group effort, so if you would like to help, email us at hello@pragmatistfoundation.com.

V2 of The Pragmatist's Guide to Life

The Pragmatist's Guide to Life was first published over half a decade ago. It has since spent over a year as the bestselling book in the world under Amazon's Agnostic category (though the book equally supports atheistic and religious perspectives) and has seen four sequels (with one even topping the Wall Street Journal's bestseller list)—becoming the first of a Pragmatist's Guide series. (So far, this series includes Pragmatist's Guides to Life, Relationships, Sexuality, Governance, and Crafting Religion.)

While the Guide to Life covers the most important topics of any book in the Pragmatist's Guide series, it also has the lowest rating on Amazon. In response, we have re-written it to shore up some of the first edition's shortcomings, also redesigning the interior of the print version in an effort to make it easier to read.

The Pragmatist's Guide to Life is a response to the extant education system's failure to provide a framework for developing independent answers to life's most important questions:

- What should I optimize for in life?
- How do I know what is true?
- Who should I be?

Sure, college philosophy courses highlight these questions, but in the same breath, present *others'* answers, sparing students the burden of finding their own conclusions. We provide a framework helping people develop answers using evidence, ideologies, and experiences they collect themselves.

The problem with this framework turned out to be twofold. First, a portion of the readership really wanted to be spoon-fed an answer. Readers frequently wrote: "I loved the book. What is the right answer?" (Cue yet another head slap moment for us). This book exists to encourage people to think through this stuff for themselves, but the natural human inclination (one we share) to look for an authority figure is difficult to overcome. On the plus side, we must have done a good job writing the book if readers feel compelled to ask us after reading it.

Some of our favorite negative reviews and angry emails assume we are trying to push an agenda that does not align with our personal beliefs. For example, one reader thought that we, fairly secular people, had written the book to secretly convert atheists to Christianity. We cannot think of a better indication that we effectively shielded readers from our own personal biases.

The second problem is less nuanced: The topic is boring if you don't love it—and if you *do* love it, you have likely thought through >70% of what the book explores. We made an effort to make the book more engaging for both groups of readers.

Finally, while this book lists Simone and Malcolm as authors, that is something of a lie. A team of about thirty editors—as well post-publication readers—made significant contributions. Whenever someone emails us with a suggested change or criticizes a part of the book in a review or email (we admittedly prefer the latter), we revisit the manuscript to make corrections. If you can think of a way to make this guide better, please contact us! Pragmatist's Guides are a collaborative effort with the goal of helping people be more intentional with their actions, identities, and beliefs about the world.

Why Bother?

Is genocide a good thing?

If you don't think genocide is good, why not? Your reaction to this question may be one of disbelief. You might be thinking, "How can you even ASK if genocide is a good thing?! OBVIOUSLY killing innocent people is wrong!" And you probably wouldn't be alone in that reaction.

Our society tells us genocide is wrong, that killing innocent people is wrong, and that racism is wrong. However, if you believe these things only or primarily because the culture in which you grew up told you they were obviously true, then you hold little moral authority over someone who participated in genocide, because the culture in which *they* grew up in told them genocide was a moral imperative.

If you took an average of cultures across human history—the things that most people in most places were raised to believe were true—you would have a culture that believed women were lesser beings than men, that some people are born better than others, that freedom of thought is not a right, and that when you conquer a city, it is perfectly moral to rape, kill, and enslave as many civilians as you want. Why were most cultures in human history wrong, whereas the time and place that you just happen to be born into correct? If you want to believe, with any intellectual integrity, that the culture you were born into or the counterculture that accepted you is more correct than others, you need to develop your own reasons why.

What you believe is a choice you can make—*independently, for yourself*. If you are reading this book, chances are you have already made your choice and have developed some system of thought-out beliefs about what is worth living for and why. The framework presented in this book will help you structure your beliefs and engage you with choices you may not have known you had. This book will also help you to build a foundation that ensures your life and actions align with what you have decided to believe.

Building this system for yourself will not always be pleasant. There will be moments when you set down the book thinking: "This is difficult to think about! This book is just too dense! Life has worked for me so far. I am done with this!"

This book was *not* written to be fun or a joy to consume. It was written to make you a better person. Many books that claim to be about some form of "self-improvement" are in reality collections of pleasant platitudes and stories that make you feel powerful while merely affirming beliefs you already kind of had. Much like fad diets and miracle cures that promise easy fixes to tough problems, "comfortable" self-improvement books leave you utterly unchanged and unimproved.

Most self-improvement books are written with the goal of selling more books. They achieve this by offering you the smallest suggested improvements necessary to allow you to feel good about the person you have allowed yourself to become so that you are likely to recommend them to others. We, brave reader, take no money from the sale of this book. *This book is only designed to help make you a better person.*

Rather than spoon-feed you pre-established beliefs, this book is designed to make you think, challenge your conceptions about the world, and develop a stronger personal system of beliefs without giving you any pre-packaged answers. Challenging personal beliefs is neither easy nor fun or pleasant, but it is a necessary step toward becoming an actualized human being.

The Framework

There are four steps to gaining ownership and intentionality over your personal identity and beliefs:

1. Determining your objective function
What is the purpose of my life?
2. Determining your ideological tree
How do I best fulfill that purpose?
3. Determining your personal identity
Who do I want to be?
4. Determining your public identity
How do I want others to think of me?

The four chapters of this guide walk you through a framework for exploring every nook and cranny of these questions in detail, but before we dive in, here is a broad overview of each step.

A Brief Introduction to Step 1: Determine Your Objective Function

Your objective function is a statement of whatever you are trying to maximize with/in your life. It is the metric by which you judge whether an action is a good or bad thing to undertake.

Typically, an objective function represents a desire to maximize whatever group of things you believe has intrinsic value. These things may involve personal happiness, pleasing God, reducing suffering in others, or any number of other things people believe have value.

Anything you do that serves your objective function is a "good" thing to do from your perspective and anything that hinders your objective function is a "bad" thing to do. Because of this, deciding your objective function is perhaps the single most important decision of your life. Your objective function sets the metric by which you judge all other decisions. Any person thinking with clarity should be referencing their objective function before any major decision.

We use the term "objective function" and not "purpose" in part because it allows for more flexibility in how you define what you want to achieve with your life. Specifically, while a purpose is commonly conceptualized as a singular goal, an objective function should be thought of as a weighted combination of the things you believe hold intrinsic value.

It requires more intellectual honesty to explore the concept of an objective function than it does to explore the concept of purpose. If asked about their purpose, a person may say they want to maximize their own happiness and that of others, whereas if asked their objective function they would have to say they value their own happiness five times as much as the happiness of others.

Should this person happen to live in a first-world country and follow through on their claimed beliefs, they would almost certainly benefit others more than 5X themselves by giving all their money to help children in the developing world. That they don't means either their stated beliefs should be altered (i.e., they actually value their own happiness 1000X that of other people), alter their actions, or accept that they choose to live a systematically immoral life. Of course, if someone alters their objective function just to make it easier to maximize without making radical changes to their lifestyle, they will need to do some pretty serious self-reflection.

This chapter of the guide will help you determine your objective function by exploring what you believe has intrinsic value. To help you consider intrinsic values that may fit well with you, we will present you with the most common conclusions people make. Each intrinsic value we introduce is accompanied by thought experiments, arguments for and against, a discussion of tough implications, and important points of consideration.

A Brief Introduction to Step 2: Determine Your Ideological Tree

The complex decisions we have to make on a daily basis do not allow us to simply reference an objective function and reach a "correct answer."

Two people who believe that pleasing God—or maximizing the ongoing viability of the human species—is the only thing of intrinsic value may decide on entirely different and contradictory paths of action in order to achieve that goal. This happens because these two people have different ideological trees.

Within this guide, we define an ideology as a hypothesis about how the world works that you utilize to maximize your objective function. For example, if your objective function is to relieve suffering in others, then one of your ideologies might be socialism because you hypothesize that socialism is an effective means of relieving suffering in others.

Ideologies exist within a branching hierarchy—an ideological tree—in which some ideologies are strictly subservient to others. An ideological tree may have Southern Baptism at its root with its political branch starting with representative democracy, followed by the Republican party, followed by a particular presidential candidate. The reason we think of ideology as a tree is that it helps us contextualize that some ideologies, e.g., "my belief that we should elect X candidate for president," may be directly subservient to other beliefs, e.g., "I believe that Y political party is the best path forward for our country." The further down the tree an ideology is for you, the more other ideologies rely on its correctness and therefore the more it is worth expending mental energy on ensuring it is correct.

In this framework, ideologies are hypotheses about how the world works and as hypotheses we should always be open to evidence that disproves them. You should always be aware of what type of evidence would be necessary for you to alter a particular path in your ideological tree. If you hypothesize that socialism is the best political system for relieving suffering, what standard of information is required for you to change your mind? Might that information already exist in the world? Have you tried to seek it out? Where might you find it?

Almost as important as our objective function is the "standard of evidence" we choose when building our ideological tree. One person may view a shift in the consensus of the scientific community as sufficient evidence that a chosen ideology is wrong while another may be willing to dismiss the consensus of the scientific community in the face of a personal experience.

This chapter will drill into the various standards of evidence a person may choose, the various advantages and disadvantages of each, and methods for maintaining an up-to-date ideological tree. We all know someone whose ideological tree ossified with age or through intellectual stagnation—someone who became resistant to new ideas or the concept that their present views of the world could be wrong. None of us wants to be that person. We all want to be able to change how we view the world in light of new information. This chapter will provide you with the framework you need to ensure your ideological tree never ossifies.

A Brief Introduction to Step 3: Determine Your Personal Identity

You get to choose who you are.
Who you decide to be should be an informed decision designed to maximize your objective

function.

The human brain is not capable of referencing an objective function and ideological tree every time it determines whether to reach for a donut, how to respond to a question, or what to post to Facebook. Most of our lives are lived in a sort of autopilot. This autopilot is driven by the type of person we have allowed ourselves to become in response to the serendipitous events we have experienced in life.

It is tempting to say, "I am perfect the way I am now" or "I can't change who I am," but both of these statements are patently false. Who you are now is a Franken-identity pieced together by experiences you have been randomly subjected to throughout your life. A personal identity you consciously create is truer to you than a self-identity created by random events.

To build your personal identity, you must take stock of your personal beliefs, strengths, and weaknesses to determine how they can best be leveraged in pursuit of your objective function. You must consciously decide who you are and who you are not. To assist you in this endeavor, we discuss the psychology and neuroscience behind the way we understand ourselves, experience emotions, maintain long-term change in ourselves, and relate to our goals to help you build an autopilot for yourself that keeps your behavior in line with your goals.

A Brief Introduction to Step 4: Determine Your Public Identity

When you rebuild yourself to be the type of person you want to be, there are two versions of you that must be constructed:

1. The "you" that exists within your own mind
2. The "you" that exists in the minds of other people

The act of building yourself is akin to the act of building a house. A guide to building houses that focused only on interior design would look silly. Likewise, someone who paid to have a house built for them would be pretty upset if, upon their arrival, their architect explained to them that no work had been done on the outside of the house because "that's not the part you see."

You may be asking: "I want people to see me for who I really am. Why can't I just show people my internal character?" The fact is, even if they could read your mind, it wouldn't help them build a picture of who you are as a person.

Stop and think for a moment: if someone spent five hours yesterday from noon to 5:00pm reading your mind, would they have a good picture of who you really are? Probably not. Now consider how many people in the last six months have spent over five hours trying to get to know you *without* the ability to read your mind. Getting to know "who you really are" is a treat reserved for only your closest and longest friends who make up the vast minority of individuals you will ever interact with.

Asking why you can't just force people to see you the way you see yourself is akin to the developers of a video game asking why they can't just put the game's code on the box, because that is what the game "really is" after all. If game developers just slapped source code on product boxes, most game box covers would look boring, overly complicated, and nearly identical.

This section explores the systems individuals use to process, store, and sort information about people they meet. Using this information, you will be guided through the process of building a public persona—the marketing box art of your chosen internal character—that harnesses these systems in order to help you achieve your objective function.

Always remember that everyone is the protagonist of their own story. This means that you, dear reader, are a supporting character in the eyes of every human being you will meet. In the story of your life, you are magnificent protagonist, but to play a meaningful role in others' narratives, you are best suited if you paint yourself as a compelling supporting character. Writing yourself as a supporting character in your own narrative is depressingly belittling to your potential while attempting to cast yourself as a protagonist in the life of someone else is psychotically narcissistic.

In short, when building yourself, it is important to both build who you want to be in your own eyes and who you want to be in the eyes of others.

How Applied Pragmatic Thought Relates to Religion, Atheism, and Philosophers

Applied pragmatic thought is a non-denominational method for increasing the intentionality of one's beliefs and life, regardless of whether these beliefs are atheistic or religious in origin.

This framework is, however, strictly opposed to using prefabricated "philosophical" belief sets as a crutch.

While you read this guide, **you will feel a natural urge to avoid having to think.** By default, whether we like to admit it or not, we tend to prefer being told what to believe or what arguments we should use to defend what we wish were true about the world. Nobody is exempt from this urge.

Anyone with access to an internet connection, a library, or memories of an introductory philosophy class can access a wide range of philosophers from both the recent and distant past who developed pre-packaged belief sets complete with fully prepared defenses to counter arguments and challenges. Building core beliefs about the world based on the arguments of philosophers is like trying to get in shape using liposuction and plastic surgery. You may look polished after the procedure, but you will have built no foundation. Having earned nothing for yourself, you will ultimately revert to your old habits.

If turning to pre-packaged philosophies is akin to getting liposuction, leveraging the framework presented in this guide is like signing up for a gym membership. Rather than artificially applying beliefs to you, we will act as your personal trainers and spotters, helping you to build and strengthen your own beliefs without doing the heavy lifting for you.

Along with a lack of personal mental effort and commitment, reliance on prepackaged beliefs carries with it the hazard of obscure vocabulary, which can slot you into potentially constraining categories, alienate you from others, and obscure your ability to truly understand what you are talking about.

For example, when trying to understand what you believe about the world, you may tumble down a Wikipedia hole and land on something like Epicureanism. At first glance, you may see Epicureanism as restrained version of an objective function focused on "maximizing personal positive emotions" and begin identifying as an Epicurean without realizing you are saying you identify with a worldview rather than just an objective function (while Epicureanism has an objective function it is a lot more than that, it is a pre-packaged worldview complete with a set of base ideologies). These prepackaged zero-thought worldviews are the microwavable dinners of identity.

Worse still is the way one can use their prepackaged buzzwords, concepts, and fallacies to create a sense of false superiority over people with whom you are communicating, which can ultimately prevent others from understanding your arguments. Ironically, obscure vocabulary may prevent you from appreciating that others' viewpoints may be more sound and valid than your own, despite their lack of fancy vocabulary.

Chances are you have, on several occasions, witnessed someone using fancy or obscure terminology to try to win or end an argument without actually thinking about the issue at hand. Chances are these people have not been very effective at changing your views. In our never-ending quest to avoid reflecting on our position in the world, there is no greater armor preventing communication than obscure terminology.

Finally, if you have reached this part of the book and are disappointed to find we won't be talking about Pragmatism, the philosophical movement of the late 1800s popularized by William James and John Dewey (or any of its modern manifestations, such as neo-classical pragmatism or analytical pragmatism), then please accept our sincerest apologies. This book is using the word "pragmatic" in the vernacular, which runs contrary to what most would consider to be an obscure, pedantic philosophical movement. (No offense to the philosophical movement; we are genuinely great admirers of it. Still, objectively speaking, most people would consider a lesser-known philosophical school of thought to be excessively academic and stuffy, which is the antithesis of the definition of the word pragmatic).

Avoiding fancy vocabulary is not easy. Even as we wrote this guide, we found ourselves relying on philosophical terms as a crutch and had to meticulously remove them. Do not fall into this trap.

Step 1: Define Your Objective Function

ob·jec·tive func·tion
noun: objective function
(in linear programming) the function that it is desired to maximize or minimize.

Our objective function is the thing we attempt to maximize or minimize in/with our lives. It is the thing we use when determining optimal actions to take. It is the measuring stick by which we judge the "correctness" of our actions and decisions.

To build your objective function, you must first define what you believe has intrinsic value, then organize these intrinsically valuable things relative to each other.

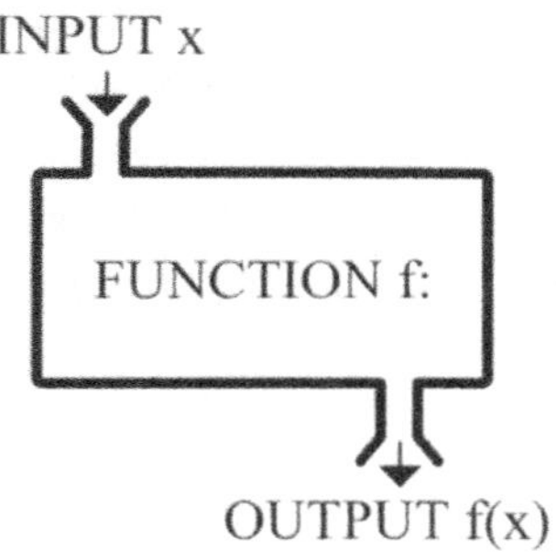

A function transforms a wide variety of inputs into an output in a systematic way. An objective function is a function designed to optimize for a certain objective. Having an objective function allows you to take in a wide variety of inputs and know what course of action you should take.

For example, you may decide you believe that both maximizing your own positive emotional state and spreading positive emotions to others has intrinsic value, but that your own emotional state is three times more valuable than the emotional states of others. By knowing that this is what you believe, you can take a set of inputs like: "*I have a dollar, if I give this dollar to person X, I estimate there is an 80% probability they will gain ten times the happiness from this dollar than I could*" and come to a confident conclusion about what course of action you should take: "*therefore, given my objective function I should give this dollar to person X.*"

An intrinsic value cannot be proven wrong in the same way an ideology can. Because an ideology (as we are defining it in this book) is a hypothesis about how to maximize an objective function, something could happen that falsifies that hypothesis. Objective functions, on the other hand, are judgment calls. Ultimately, no one can tell you that yours is "wrong."

We understand the term "objective function" is not a simple English term people commonly use and that, in this sense, it violates our pledge to avoid special vocabulary. This is one of the only places in this guide in which we use an obscure term as opposed to something more mainstream. We would not do this unless we felt it were absolutely necessary. The mainstream term we would use, "purpose," has a lot of baggage and preconceived notions attached to it, which muddle its place in our lives.

There are several problems with the term "purpose" that do not arise when we use the term "objective function":

- Purpose is often taken to be a single, discrete thing one is trying to achieve, which is unnecessarily limiting.
- Purpose is taken to be something that is concretely "finishable." Thus, there is often no winning in life when one has a purpose: "finishing" a purpose before dying indicates wasted potential and failing to "finish" a purpose before dying means failure.
- Purpose is often used to refer to an ideology (e.g., to defend the American way of life) instead of a thing of intrinsic value (e.g., maximizing human liberty and self- determination).

The term "objective function" and our particular use of the term "ideology" will be the only two unique terms used in this guide.

Why Do I Need to Think Through an Objective Function?

You may be thinking "I have a set of beliefs that work for me. Why question them?" or "I just don't care. This isn't a question that is important to me."

"What is your objective function?" is the single most important question in your life. Your answer to this question will be used to judge the fidelity of every decision you make. Whether an action or decision you make is "good" or "bad" from your perspective depends entirely on what you believe is intrinsically good or bad in the world.

Throughout history, there have been many times during which mainstream ethics promoted presently unthinkable actions such as slavery, recreational rape, and genocide.

You may think: "Sure, societies condoned unethical things in the past, but our modern society doesn't do that anymore."

Consider that someone in the slaveholding South would have said the exact same thing and 100% believed it. "We live in an age of enlightenment," this person might proclaim, going on to discuss how unethical people were in the past and how they had risen above those barbaric practices. "In ancient Greece, terrible sins such as homosexuality were allowed," they might argue, "but we do not allow such things in this modern day."

Ethics does not move in only one direction as this example demonstrates. Rather than progress incrementally toward acceptance, social norms have wavered between periods of dehumanizing and accepting the LGBT community.

You cannot know if you are a modern version of a nineteenth century slave owner if you are not willing to look at your value system critically. It is tempting to assume that nothing in society's modern morality is remotely equitable to slavery, but depending on your beliefs about what has intrinsic value, this is not necessarily true.

Many frameworks for understanding the world might view anything from abortion to the industrial slaughter of animals for consumption as horrendously unethical. It is entirely plausible that in a future society capable of synthetic meat production, our present industrial slaughter of animals will be seen as terrifyingly evil on a scale equal to any past atrocity in human history (especially if they don't see a distinction between the emotional state of humans and animals). Whether we choose to eat meat today depends on our objective functions and how they relate to the lives of animals and plants. If you do not believe the life or experiences of a cow have inherent value, you can enjoy a hamburger with a clear conscience. However, if you do conclude a cow's feelings have value, you may need to change your actions and lifestyle.

We wish there were more concise way to reason through objective functions while still giving an even shake to a broad range of perspectives.
If you find this section tedious, skip it—it is not indicative of the following three steps. Even if you find this type of thing interesting, consider skipping around to the parts that are most relevant to you.

The Uniqueness of Objective Functions to the Human Condition

Over time, people have found thousands of different ways to define how human consciousness is differentiated from the way animals interact with the world. We instinctively want to define what makes our conscious experience of the world unique. We would like to take this opportunity to throw our proverbial hat into the ring. The one thing a human can do that an animal cannot is choose its own objective function.

Let us consider a dog named Sparky. Sparky probably has a mental landscape in which he exists and in which he feels pain, pleasure, pride, or boredom. Sparky certainly creates hypotheses about how the world works while learning from those around him. Sparky can even make choices about how best to achieve what he wants. The one thing Sparky can't do is choose his objective function. Like most animals, Sparky has had his objective function bred into him: he wants to eat, procreate, carry out his training (emotional conditioning), and—thanks to centuries of selective breeding—please and be of service to his human family. (We are by no means trying to trivialize this emotion in dogs. This emotional drive is likely more powerfully felt than the emotion humans call love, because stronger selective pressures have created it.)

Sparky has the capacity to think: "How do I maximize positive emotions?" but he cannot question whether he should want to maximize his positive emotions.

The ability to ask: "Should I try to optimize the objective function that is a combination of inbred traits and conditioning I have experienced, or should I attempt to optimize for something else?" and then ask: "Why should I try to optimize for that other thing?" is a uniquely human capability.

A human who chooses not to exercise their ability to choose what she wants from life is denying the single aspect of their consciousness that differentiates them from an animal.

A Note on Challenges to Objective Functions

Because we are firmly against pushing one belief system over another belief system, we make a point of trying to provide the most simple, compelling argument possible against all belief systems discussed. Whenever we explain why someone might support a specific objective function, we also attempt to create a strong argument against that objective function.

Often these arguments take the form of thought experiments: analogies or forced decisions meant to determine if you really believe what you think you believe. These thought experiments are typically tailored to the belief system of a person we expect might hold such an objective function (e.g., a challenge to an objective function that would likely only be held by atheists may include the presupposition that evolution is true and that emotional states are an emergent property of brain states, whereas an objective function that an evangelical Christian might hold will not include such assumptions in its discussion). For example, when challenging you to carefully consider an objective function oriented around maximizing personal good feelings, we may ask:

If you could live in a human-sized tube that would make you live twice as long as you would outside the tube and pump you full of good feelings that were more diverse and more enjoyable than any feeling you could experience outside the tube, would you choose to drop everything about your life this instant and commit to the tube for the rest of your life, despite the fact that you would lose all contact with friends and family and never leave the tube again?

This challenge forces you to ask yourself if there is not something else more important to you than this specific objective function. The challenge is not meant to question or insult the value of the objective function itself, nor is it meant to deride anyone who should choose it.

It is very important you do not try to "cheat" a thought experiment by arguing about the challenge's details, because doing so enables you to avoid a difficult but necessary decision. By answering the question with a cheat answer such as, "No, I wouldn't live in the happiness tube because it is a drug and I may get addicted to it," or "I would get used to feeling positive emotions all the time and they would no longer feel good after a short period," you are avoiding the substance of the question and not allowing yourself to be meaningfully challenged. The point of the question is to force you to reflect on whether or not you would actually accept perfect emotional optimization over all other things.

What Has Inherent Value?

An Overview of What People Choose to Maximize with their Objective Functions

To establish your objective function, you must make a judgment call about what does and does not have intrinsic value, as your values are what your objective function is meant to maximize.
There are five broad categories people fall into when determining what does or does not have intrinsic value:

1. Nothing has intrinsic value
2. Something has innate, intrinsic value
3. Something has intrinsic value, but they don't know what
4. Religious tradition determines what has intrinsic value
5. Desired self-perception determines what has intrinsic value

Finally, we will review proclivities, things that you may want in your life even though you recognize they have no intrinsic value.

Nothing has Intrinsic Value

Many conclude that nothing has intrinsic value. The arguments in favor of this belief are so simplistic and apparent they do not warrant enumeration.

The core argument against this category of belief system is that if there is even the tiniest possibility that *anything* might have intrinsic value, it is best to go forward assuming that thing *does* have intrinsic value.

Consider the following thought experiment:
You have just survived a plane crash in the desert. You have no idea where you are or whether civilization is close by or entirely out of reach. You can see nothing on the horizon but sand. You know for an absolute fact that no search parties will come to save you (perhaps in this thought experiment there are laws against saving people from plane crashes or entering the desert you crashed in).[1] What is the most logical course of action if your goal is staying alive? Is it just to stay at the crash site, where you know you will die, or is it worth traveling in any random direction in the hope of finding something? If you choose to move, you are still likely to die, but there is also a probability—albeit a small one—that you will find water, food, or even a small camp, and will survive. What do you do: stay put

---

[1] If it wasn't for this addendum the most logical course of action would be to stay with the plane. Remember, this is a thought experiment not a guide for surviving in the desert.

and die, or leave the crash site to see what you might find?

In the above thought experiment it is only logical to stay with the plane if you are absolutely certain that doing so would not decrease your probability of surviving (assuming you are optimizing for survival, which to digest the above thought experiment with intellectual honesty, you must assume). Because we know that staying with the plane has a 0% probability of survival, it only is logical to stay with the plane if you are certain there is also a 0% probability of survival no matter which direction you might take. (A known 0% chance of survival no matter what you do is very different from a hypothesized 0% chance of survival.)

Similarly, it is only logical to live your life assuming nothing has intrinsic value if you are categorically certain nothing has intrinsic value. If you live life assuming nothing has intrinsic value, there is a 0% possibility your existence will have had any meaning or value. If, however, there is even a slight chance that something might have intrinsic value, no matter how slight that chance might be, that thing is worth pursuit.

There are four exceptions to the above argument:

1. An individual could offer some iteration of the "Pascal's Mugging" counter argument, which we discuss below.

2. An individual could argue that the analogy is flawed, as even by living as if nothing has value an individual still might stumble into a meaningful life. While this is true, unless we have access to no meaningful information about what does or does not have value, the probability of living a life of value will always be higher when attempting to do so.

To hold this counter argument, you must believe that we have no way to infer what may have intrinsic value. A person making this argument would also have to hold that preventing suffering is just as likely to maximize intrinsic value as maximizing the number of things painted purple.

3. An individual could take exception to the plane analogy's assumption that the stranded individual's goal should be survival, which, in the analogy, equates to a life of value. In essence, such a person claims that someone who knew what was necessary to live a meaningful existence may discard said information and instead choose to live a meaningless existence. We have trouble believing someone would make this argument as anything other than a thought experiment.
4. An individual could argue that a life which *might* have intrinsic value is not the same as a life that *does* have intrinsic value. To this, we would reply that a life with a 1% probability of having intrinsic value still has infinitely more intrinsic value than a life we are *certain* lacks intrinsic value. If one is attempting to live a

meaningful existence, it is worth it to do whatever you think has the highest probability of making your life meaningful, even if that probability is very low.

In short, to hold the belief that nothing has intrinsic value, it is not enough to think it is very likely that nothing has intrinsic value. You have concluded with certainty, through a logical thought process, that nothing has intrinsic value.

People who choose to believe they are certain nothing has intrinsic value typically choose one of the following objective functions:

- Maximizing personal good feelings: If nothing matters, you might as well default to what your biology tells you to do (which is, to feel good).
- Moving society forward: If you do not feel good about being someone who only seeks pleasure, you might instead choose to move society forward primarily to cultivate a sense of superiority over others who you see as pursuing more animalistic instincts.
- Serving one's role in society: You may, upon determining that nothing has intrinsic value, default to maximizing non-intrinsic values such as your role in society or family traditions—be it serving in the military, being part of the family business, or just being the best possible elementary school traffic cop you can be.

Pascal's Mugging

A mugger steps out in front of you and tells you that if you don't send him all your money, he will open a dimensional portal and kill a random person. Push back and he then threatens to kill a hundred people, then a thousand, then a million. By the above logic, at some point even the slight possibility he follows through should logically become enough to motivate you to give him your money because that slight probability is being multiplied by all the potential lives lost. Common sense would suggest that line of reasoning is ridiculous . . . or at least that is how the Pascal's Mugging thought experiment goes.

While this thought experiment is meant to show the flaw in utility maximization, it kind of sucks for three reasons:

- Common sense suggests the above argument is ridiculous because it recognizes that raising the number of people the mugger threatens to kill does not actually increase the odds that he will kill more people. If a kid tells you they might live five hundred years if you eat a magical marshmallow while if you don't, you will live a billion years, you recognize that there is no method of action for that statement to have an effect on reality—the same should be true with Pascal's Mugging.
- If Pascal's Mugging plays out in a scenario were raising the claimed small-probability threat really *does* increase the number of people who might

be hurt, the fact that common sense says the logical answer is wrong does not make it wrong. Common sense is merely a gut instinct we evolved to help us in situations that frequently occurred in our ancestral setting and impacted the number of surviving children our ancestors had. There are some types of questions that common sense will consistently get wrong—questions that deal with scenarios we never would have experienced in an evolutionary context. Common sense flounders when contending with low-probability, high-impact events.

- The Pascal's Mugging scenario assumes the asset being given up has some value to the person being mugged. A person who believes that nothing has intrinsic value does not believe they are giving up anything by choosing to live their life in a specific way.

Considerations if you decide you believe nothing has intrinsic value

Even if you decide nothing has intrinsic value, you must still define an objective function for yourself. Deciding that "nothing matters" doesn't absolve you from the logical imperative to be intentional in whatever you do decide to focus on in life and how you pursue it.

Something Has Innate Intrinsic Value

In this section, we will discuss intrinsic values that may exist as part of an individual's objective function independent of religious traditions.

While these values are independent from religious traditions, they are not exclusively atheist. For example, a Christian may think human suffering is intrinsically bad, independent of what his or her religious tradition says (in fact, the classic paradox, which asks: "How does suffering exist in a world with a good God?" presumes that even religious individuals believe suffering is inherently of negative value independent of religious tradition).

How does something become imbued with intrinsic value?

Before we can delve into various things an individual may believe have intrinsic value, we will take a quick detour to discuss the two core ways a thing may be imbued with intrinsic value. We can conclude something has either *absolute* intrinsic value or *relative* intrinsic value.

Absolute Intrinsic Value

Something of absolute intrinsic value is something that has value regardless of the perspective of the entity deciding whether it has value (in this case that entity is you). Something of absolute intrinsic value has value somehow imbued into its very nature. This is the way we normally think about the concept of intrinsic value. The classic example of something with absolute intrinsic value would be a deity (God, Allah, Yahweh, etc.).

Relative Intrinsic Value

Something with relative intrinsic value gains value through the nature of its relationship to the entity deciding whether it has value (in this case, that entity is you).

Most relative intrinsic value arguments are versions of the same base argument.

- You must have value from your own perspective
- Therefore, there is intrinsic value in maximizing good for yourself.

While this may seem like a simple argument, it can manifest itself in a plethora of ways depending on how you define "yourself" and "good."

By extending the definition of yourself or by focusing on aspects of yourself, you can come to wildly different conclusions about what has intrinsic value. For example, at its broadest interpretation, you may say:

- I am an entity made of stuff.
- Therefore, from my perspective, things made of stuff have value when contrasted with things that do not exist.

- Therefore, something that caused the end of stuff (the universe) would be an intrinsically negative event from my perspective and from the perspective of all other entities made of stuff.

While the relative intrinsic value argument may seem strong, it can be discounted out of hand if you categorically reject the argument that an entity has intrinsic value from its own perspective (i.e., that you have intrinsic value from the perspective of yourself).

Positive Personal Emotions

Maximizing positive personal emotions is most individuals' "default" intrinsic value. To some extent, the pursuit of happiness is an aspect of almost everyone's objective function, whether or not one sees it as having objective value.

Humans evolved[2] emotions as a tool for controlling behavior—thus emotions are quite powerful. You feel something as a positive emotion (whether it be

---

[2] We mention evolution because it is relevant to almost anyone who holds this value set. Those who do not believe in evolution also likely believe God has absolute inherent value and therefore would probably not consider positive personal emotions as having inherent value in the first place, as a true believer's objective function would naturally revolve around serving God.

love, lust, or a sense of accomplishment from a job well done) because humans who experienced these emotions in the past had a higher probability of surviving long enough to reproduce and raise children who in turn survived and reproduced. Whether they be love, envy, or the joy from a job well done, all emotions exist for this one reason.

At their core, emotions are neurological states. They exist as a specific configuration of neural pathways and levels of neurotransmitters. We even currently have the technology to directly induce complicated emotions through chemicals or direct stimulation of parts of the brain (See: transcranial magnetic stimulation, a.k.a. TMS).

These two facts alone are enough to convince many that positive feelings are too trivial to have intrinsic value. The fact that emotions are mechanical, chemically induced states meant to help us pass on our genes certainly makes it difficult to believe that any specific individual's positive emotional states are of *absolute* intrinsic value.

That said, it is not incredibly difficult to conclude that from a relative perspective, positive feelings have inherent value. If we are our minds and our minds perceive certain states as being superior to others, those states may have intrinsic value to us.

There is a tendency among those who by default conclude that personal positive emotions have intrinsic value to rank some emotions as having more intrinsic value than others. Specifically, they elevate emotions that require significant effort to achieve and/or lead us to become better members of society, such as love and the satisfaction we get from accomplishing difficult tasks (as opposed to positive emotions we get from eating, sex, sleeping in, etc.).

For individuals who feel this way, it is useful to determine whether it is the emotions themselves that have value, whether true value lies in the struggle to achieve these emotions, or whether the value of these emotions lies in beneficial results for society. This can be achieved by returning to the thought experiment we engaged earlier:

You are given the option to spend the rest of your life in a tube that enables you to live twice as long as you would outside of the tube. The tube pumps your brain full of the chemicals necessary to constantly feel whatever emotional state it is that you value the most (or whatever series of emotions you think has the most value in exactly the amounts you deem as having the most value). This tube will better serve an objective function to maximize positive feelings than any life you could live independently. Will you choose to live in the tube, even though it means foregoing normal life and leaving everyone you have known? (The tube would be able to maximize the feelings you got from the interactions you used to have with these individuals.)

It is easy to dodge the intent of this question by claiming that the emotions wouldn't feel so good over time, or the emotions wouldn't be "real" and thus do not count. Do not do this. These sorts of cheating answers rob you of a learning experience that helps you understand what you really believe about the world. The intention of this thought experiment is to determine whether positive personal emotions really *are* what you want to maximize with your life, or if there is something that matters more (not to determine whether you actually want to live in a tube).

If you have trouble with the above scenario and do not understand why, ask yourself: If you had a button that would prevent you from ever feeling a negative feeling again, would you press it? If your reaction is "no," because negative feelings are useful for some reason, focus on whatever that reason is. Does this reason have a deeper intrinsic value to it than the experience of positive personal emotions? If you feel this reason is more important to you than not ever having to feel a negative emotion again, then you are tacitly admitting to yourself there is something more valuable to you than your emotional state. Why is it more important?

You may try to dodge the intent of the question with some platitude about how negative emotions make positive emotions sweeter. However, such an assertion is really just saying that negative emotions help one more effectively maximize the experience of positive emotions, in which case, we ask you to attempt the same thought experiment with the concession that somehow this button will amplify the experience of positive emotions to offset this effect.

Considerations if you decide you believe that positive personal emotions have intrinsic value

Even if you decide to dedicate your life to maximizing positive personal emotions, allowing your emotions to drag you around like a dog on a leash is a terrible method for maximizing your positive emotions.

Those seeking to maximize a positive state must remain aware that chasing elevated emotional states in the moment will almost always lead to a lower overall emotional state in the long run. Sometimes this is obvious. Were you to sit around all day eating Doritos, drinking Mountain Dew, and indulging in your hobby, you may feel great in the short run, but after a few days of this you would feel gross and awful. This is a feeling anyone who has been unemployed or taken a long vacation knows all too well: You think having all the free time in the world to do something you enjoy in the moment will feel great, but once you have that time, that happiness fades and the activity becomes routine.

Much of the lost luster of short-term pleasures is due to overlay states. These states are discussed in chapter three, which explores ways to maximize desired emotional states. Many of the emotional states we chase are also heavily romanticized by mainstream culture (hence our interest in them) and pursuing them leads to less satisfaction than one would expect based on the hype.

Let us examine the worst offender here—love—to demonstrate this point. First, we should acknowledge that (if you assume a scientific perspective) love evolved to facilitate long-term pair bonding and increase the likelihood that an individual will protect and raise viable children. In other words, people in the past who felt love were more likely to have kids who survived long enough to reproduce themselves. Because of this, your body will begin to feel love for anyone that your body, on an animalistic level, believes has the potential to become your long-term partner.

Your body is not the best matchmaker. It can even be tricked into falling in love. For example, studies conducted by Author Aran demonstrated a simple experimental task could be used to cause two individuals to fall in love in under an hour (this task was so effective that some of Author's test subjects, who had never met before the experiment, eventually married).

If you want to maximize the amount of love you will feel in your life, allowing a feeling of love to guide your choices about a lifelong partner is a poor strategy. In a 2012 study, happiness and love ratings after ten years of marriage were equal to those of arranged marriages; however, divorce rates in love marriages are 40-50% while divorce rates in arranged marriages are 4-6%. When you adjust for survivorship bias, you are more likely to maximize the love you feel in your life by letting someone else—who is not operating under the influence of love—choose who you marry. In an ideal scenario, you will decide for yourself who you marry without allowing the decision to be influenced by love. Just be aware that evidence indicates you have a higher probability of living a life with more love in it if you do not allow love to influence major life decisions, such as who you choose to marry. (If you enjoy this topic, please check out the sequel to this book, *The Pragmatist's Guide to Relationships*—it digs into it a lot deeper.)

Finally, we have a lot of control over our emotional states. If you genuinely believe that positive emotions have inherent value in your life, then you have a moral imperative to not allow yourself to feel sad when it is within your control (i.e., pretty much any time you are not clinically depressed, in which case it would then be your moral imperative to seek clinical treatment). This means that whenever you throw yourself a personal pity party, it is your moral obligation to catch yourself and find a way to be happy about your situation. (Later in the book we explore data demonstrating the amount of emotional control people really have along with methods for improving emotional control.)

Deciding that your objective function is to maximize your emotional state is not the same as deciding that your objective function is to take the path of least resistance in life—the path your brain will try to push you towards. Maximizing an emotional state takes a lot of work and willpower. Nevertheless, by combining cold logic and repeated effort with willpower, it is remarkably possible to live a life of near constant bliss, assuming this is something you decide has inherent value. This topic will be covered in detail within Chapter 3.

Note: We do not include the path of least resistance in our lists of potential objective functions. The only argument we could think to justify it is that consciously experiencing life is inherently negative and nothing has positive value, hence one should do everything in one's power to consciously experience as little of life as possible. We don't think anyone genuinely holds that belief.

Distributed Positive Emotions

When asked in public what has intrinsic value, many people reflexively refer to distributed positive emotions—that is, making as many people happy (or content, satisfied, not in pain, etc.) as possible.

A claim that distributed positive emotional experiences have inherent value is built on the premise that a positive emotional state in a human has intrinsic value and thus there is intrinsic value in distributing positive emotions. Because of this, any criticism that may be levied against someone believing personal positive emotions are of intrinsic value can also be levied at an individual who believes distributing positive emotional states has value. This includes the accusation that positive emotional states only encourage organisms to survive and breed and that ultimately a positive emotional state is no more than a neurochemical slurry (and not something of intrinsic value).

Typically, the reason someone ends up believing that distributive positive emotions have intrinsic value is they ascribe absolute value to positive emotional states, leaving their own mental state in a non-privileged position (e.g., because they believe something about positive emotional states imbues them with intrinsic value, they must believe that positive emotions experienced by others are as valuable as positive emotions in themselves). However, an absolute perspective on positive emotions having intrinsic value forces one to decide what categories of entities' positive emotional states have intrinsic value and justify the lines one draws. Deciding whether the emotional states of cows, dogs, humans, the severely mentally disabled, aliens, artificially intelligent machines, etc., have inherent value is not as easy as it may at first seem.

Does a cow's positive emotional state have the same value as that of a human? Does a worm having its reward pathways activated have the same value as a cow being in a state of positive emotion? If you ascribe a cow or a worm's positive emotional state as having a lower value than that of a human, how do you justify this? If you justify it by saying that positive emotions scale in value based on the cognitive capacity of the entity experiencing the emotion, then you must believe that babies and disabled humans born with a lower cognitive capacity are of lower priority when one distributes positive emotional states.

One common way people answer this line of questioning is by claiming that there is a threshold of cognitive capacity and once an entity is over that threshold, it has equal value to all other entities above that threshold. In other words, once an animal is above a certain level of intelligence, it has equal rights to positive emotions as all other animals above that threshold of intelligence. If you hold this position, where do you place this intelligence threshold and why do you place it there?

Is the intelligence threshold set at the lowest limit of human cognitive capacity? If so, then you would believe some non-human apes have exactly equal value to their emotional states as humans, as the smartest non-human apes are certainly at an intelligence range higher than that of the most cognitively impaired adult humans. Also, it is suspiciously convenient that the cut off would be at the lower levels of your own species intelligence levels. Are you certain you are not allowing modern notions of political correctness to taint your perceptions of what has intrinsic value?

If you accept the above argument and conclude that the happiness of a non-human ape is of the exact same value as the happiness of a human, given that it is cheaper to maintain the happiness of a chimpanzee, is it not more cost and resource effective to keep large regions dedicated to chimpanzee farms in which they are kept as happy as possible? Such farms would be more efficient than programs to help needy humans, as ten chimpanzees can be given a great life at the cost of giving one human an average one.

However, if you *don't* use a threshold after which all things happiness have equal value, but instead use a sliding scale tied to some variable with which things with more of variable X have more intrinsic value when experiencing happiness (i.e., you hold that the value of an animal or person's emotional state scales based on something like its level of intelligence, cognitive capacity, or capacity for experiencing emotions), then consider the following thought experiment:

Would the happiness of aliens who were significantly smarter than humans (or had more of whatever X variable is) be of higher value than the happiness of humans? If a massively more intelligent species came to earth, would it be within their right to treat the human population in the same way we regard indigenous species when cutting down their habitat to grow more food in order to increase human happiness? If humans went to war with this alien species because they were exterminating us, would it not be your moral obligation to fight for the aliens?

An alternative thought experiment could go:

If you could build a super intelligent AI and design it to experience nothing but extremely high levels of positive emotions, would that satisfy your objective function?

The above problems can be escaped by taking a relative—rather than absolute—perspective when making an argument for the value of positive emotions. Specifically, an individual would either argue that entities like themselves have intrinsic value from their perspective or that they are part of a larger entity defined as the human race. This allows an individual to easily say that because the aliens are different from them, they care less about their positive emotional states and that the emotional states of animals that are more closely related to them are more valuable than those of species that are further removed. An individual holding this perspective likely also believes that their family's happiness is of higher value than individuals who are not as closely related to them.

A thought experiment that can be used to test whether you believe that distributed positive emotional states have value from a relative perspective might be:

If you could press a button that put all humans (or whatever group you consider worthy of positive emotions) into tubes that would double their lifespans and ensure they only felt happy emotions until they died, would you press that button?

If you do not press the button, is it because you believe that others may not want to live life in a happiness tube? Ultimately, you may conclude that self-determination is something with greater intrinsic value than distributive happiness.

Consider this question from a slightly different angle: If someone does not want to feel a positive emotional state, is there value in forcing one upon them? If you truly believe that distributive positive emotional states have inherent value, it should not matter what others want.

One must also ask: Does the positive mental state of an entity that you believe is immoral hold value equal to the positive mental state of a person you deem to be moral or morally neutral? For example, does the happiness of a serial killer on death row have value equal to that of an innocent, starving child in Africa? You could argue that entities that take happiness from others are less deserving of happiness themselves, but why would that be the case? Would it not be better to just kill any entity that took happiness from others instead of bothering to deny it happiness?

This brings us to our final question: Per your logic, is it best to kill an entity that will feel no positive emotions for the rest of its existence? What if any positive emotions felt by this entity will be vastly outweighed by negative emotions? What if this entity will feel mostly positive emotions, but cause so much sadness to others that it has a net negative effect on the world's happiness?

Considerations if you decide you believe that distributive positive emotions have intrinsic value

If you decide that distributed positive emotions have inherent value, as discussed above, you will need to decide whose happiness matters.
To summarize the most common choices are:

- All entities that meet a certain threshold should be distributed equal happiness.
- Entities with more of X trait should be distributed more happiness in proportion to how much of X

trait they exhibit (where X is usually intelligence or consciousness).

- Entities more closely related to you should be distributed happiness based on how "related" to you they are (the metric of "related" is flexible; it could signify individuals who think like you or individuals genetically related to you).

It can seem fussy to focus as much as we do on questions regarding whose emotional experiences matter and why (e.g., whether the experience of animals matters). However, these questions have monumental real-world implications. After formulating your position on the question, "when does the emotional state of others matter and why?" we would ask you to focus on the implications of your answer to the wellbeing of human babies. Does your answer suggest that it is worse for a human baby to feel pain than a pig? Is it worse for a human baby to feel pain than a human adult? Based on your explanation when does a human feeling pain first matter in their development (e.g., at what stage does a fetus' emotional state matter and why)?

As you can see, if you decide positive emotional states have value, it is crucial to clearly identify what entities' happiness matters and why. Based on how you answer such questions, you may find yourself living as the client of a government committing genocide on an unprecedented level (either to animals or fetuses) and knowing whether you are living under such a government is not a trivial question.

Limiting Extreme Negative Emotions

You may choose to dismiss the arguments against maximizing positive emotions by claiming that you are striving for a more restrained state of happiness. This involves arguing that while maximizing positive emotional states may lack intrinsic value, you are at least certain there is something intrinsically bad about suffering (e.g., a child starving to death), and therefore there is intrinsic value in preventing it.

If you feel inclined to agree with this perspective, then all the arguments and challenges above should be considered, but in a restrained state (i.e., pleasantness pods instead of happiness tubes).

The following thought experiment can help define your stance on this belief:

If suffering is of intrinsic negative value, is it not best to sterilize the populations of countries with high levels of suffering? If you had a button that would sterilize the entire population of the three countries with the most suffering, would you push that button? Pushing this button would certainly drastically decrease future suffering in that region (in terms of the number of people suffering), so if you choose not to push it, you will guarantee the suffering for hundreds of thousands of people. What if the button did more? Would you push the button if it painlessly killed the entire population of the three countries with the most suffering? Remember: By doing this, you would eliminate more suffering from the world in a second than you could in an entire normal lifetime.

Do not attempt to dodge the question to avoid making a choice. You either get to push the button or not push the button with the understanding that any unhappiness caused by your pushing the button will be less than the unhappiness experienced if you don't. In this scenario, helping them in any other way is not a choice available to you.

If you cannot bring yourself to push the button, is it because you see more value in having a human being be alive and in great pain than not alive at all? In this case, should you not optimize for the number of people (or animals if you value their suffering) you can have living in a region regardless of the suffering that causes? (i.e., If you believe that something being alive yet in suffering has more value than something not being alive, then your objective function would be to maximize the size of the population not to minimize suffering.)

Alternatively, you may not be able to push the button because you see self-determination as more valuable than an absence of suffering, in which case your objective function should be about the maximization of self-determination rather than the reduction of human suffering (as you view it as a strictly superior intrinsic value).

Considerations if you decide you believe that limiting extreme negative emotions has intrinsic value

Whether you believe suffering has intrinsic negative value or general positive emotions have intrinsic positive value, it is important to consider whether you ascribe equal value to the happiness of an individual alive today and the happiness of an individual in the future. This decision is crucial as it will influence the ideology you adopt (remember, in this book ideologies are defined as hypotheses on how to maximize your objective function).

For example, if the happiness of people yet to be born is of equal value to the happiness of people alive today, your efforts are almost always going to be better spent advancing technology than helping individuals who are suffering today. Better technology helps the potentially infinite stream of humans yet to be born, whereas any action to help someone today will likely only help one individual or a comparatively small population.

A question that can help ferret out if you really believe this is to ask yourself:

If you knew that humans would exist for at least another few millennia at current (or greater) population levels, would you push a button that would cause 50% of the world's population to live in chattel slavery for the rest of their lives if it decreased the number of future generations that live in extreme suffering by 10% each generation going forward?

One question we focused on in this section was: "Is it better for a person to live a life of suffering or not live at all?" A related question worth thinking through is: "Why does it matter if someone dies?"

If someone dies without feeling any pain, why is that a bad thing? Is it worse to kill someone painlessly or to torture someone for decades? What if, instead of decades, you torture someone for half an hour? The answers to questions like this greatly affect your position on fixing the world's greatest problems, such as poverty and hunger.

Freedom / Liberty / Self Determination

People who believe freedom has inherent value hold the ability of a conscious entity to do "what it wants" above all else.

Many people arrive at freedom as the thing of highest intrinsic value after realizing they cannot completely follow-through with one of the hard questions associated with another value, which would make it their moral imperative to impose this other value system on others *against their will* (like forcing happiness on other people).

The argument for self-determination mirrors the argument for general positive emotions *except* it makes the concession that general emotional states (such as happiness) either do not matter or matter less than one's ability to freely act on one's emotional state at any given time.

Anyone choosing to work freedom into their objective function will have to draw some careful boundaries before proceeding. What is "freedom," anyway?

Consider the life of an Emirati living in the UAE. He has no fear of abject poverty given the generous government welfare system, but he can't watch porn, drink alcohol, or say whatever he wants in public (we are obviously oversimplifying the laws of the country for the sake of making an argument). Is this Emirati more free than a man living in the United States, who *can* watch porn, drink alcohol, and say what he wants, but is restrained by the bounds of poverty?

What aspects of freedom have intrinsic value? Why do those aspects have intrinsic value?

If your answer is ever another intrinsic value (e.g., "The fact that freedom makes people happier gives it intrinsic value"), then freedom is *not* of intrinsic value to you. In such cases, freedom is instead a hypothesis about maximizing something else of intrinsic value.

To test your belief that freedom has intrinsic value, ask yourself:
If you could press a button that would make the world's population 15% less happy but 10% more free (by whatever metric you define freedom) would you?

If you find yourself arguing that doing so would rob people of the ability to make the decision themselves, you reveal that you are not actually driven by a fundamental belief in freedom (as this button would unquestionably make people freer), but rather a fundamental distaste for making decisions that affect other people.

Considerations if you decide you believe that freedom has inherent value

If you conclude freedom has intrinsic value, you will need to think carefully about your hypothesis in order to identify how best to achieve it. There are wildly different political ideologies regarding freedom that all claim that *their* method maximizes it, and that all other ideologies make the situation worse. It is specifically meaningful to consider questions of how much wealth an individual needs to achieve meaningful freedom and whether more powerful or less powerful governing entities are better at ensuring freedom.

Immortality / Continued Existence

There is an innate human desire not to die. From an evolutionary perspective, this is not surprising; humans that didn't have this drive would have died at much higher frequencies. Given how ingrained not wanting to die is into our subconscious, it is also not surprising that so many people conclude that some form of continuing their own existence has intrinsic value.

The argument used to come to this conclusion is almost always a relative argument and typically goes something like: "From my perspective, I have intrinsic value, thus creating more of myself in the future is a thing of intrinsic value."

This intrinsic value is unique in the vast number of contradictory forms in which it might manifest. A good thought experiment for beginning to explore this is the Ship of Theseus:

Theseus sails his ship around the Aegean Sea for many years and during his journey replaces any old planks that might be starting to rot or show signs of damage. After many months of travel, Theseus has replaced so many planks of his ship that none of the original planks remain. Is this still the same ship? What if, during the voyage, someone had been following Theseus' ship and gathering the old boards as they were discarded? What if this person rebuilt a ship that looked exactly like the Theseus' original ship, using the boards from the original ship? Which of the two ships is the real ship?

Consider that if you compare yourself today with yourself at the age of seven, you likely have almost none of the same cells, are made up of entirely different matter, and hold almost none of the same ideas. How you think about this thought experiment has implications on what "you" and "continued existence" mean to you.

We will take this opportunity to briefly discuss some of the ways people interpret themselves:

- You are your consciousness over time
- You are your body
- You are the current snapshot of your consciousness
- You are the story other people use to conceptualize you

You are your consciousness through time

In this interpretation, you are your conscious mind and seek to prolong your own conscious life as long as possible—either by downloading yourself into a computer, preserving your own body as long as possible, or freezing your brain in the hopes of someday resurrecting it. While these may sound like far-fetched ideas, they are common amongst rationalist and human+ communities.

The core issue faced by these ideologies is how much of "you" is even maintained in your consciousness over time. Given how radically we will change our beliefs throughout our lives, can we confidently assert that we, today, will be closer to whatever we become four hundred years from now than our grandchildren?

Is it really so bad that you get to remix your genetics with any individual you choose, then give the new version of yourself whatever childhood you want, thereby granting the new-and-improved "you" an opportunity to reinterpret reality with all of your guidance but none of your already-ingrained biases and flaws?

Consider the following thought experiment:
Today you are given the option to live forever and given a button that will make you feel whatever emotional state you want whenever you want, but you must get in a luxurious spaceship that will be shot into empty space with no hope of finding anything. Would you take this deal?

If you would not take this deal, why not?

Is it that you want to be able to interact with the world as an entity living as long as you can? Is it that you want to make some sort of impact on the world? If this is the case, are your resources really being optimally spent on living longer?

You are your body

In this case, "you" are defined as a bundle of genes (and not individual cells, as obviously your body itself is regularly recycled on a cellular level). To maximize your existence, you must strive to maximize the prevalence of your genetic material in the future. The core challenges to this come from the question: Is the conscious entity reading this book and making these decisions, really your body (that bundle of genes), or is your conscience not beholden to your body?

If your conscious is not beholden to your body, it makes more sense to see yourself as your ideas rather than your genetics. A tough question to ask if you believe the "you are your body" version is whether you would kill yourself today if it allowed you to spread 5% of your genetic material to everyone born in the next generation.

You are the current snapshot of your conscious mind

In this interpretation, you see yourself as a bundle of ideas trying to spread. In this case, you are the current state of your consciousness and what it contains, and the more you spread the ideas your consciousness contains, the closer you get to immortality.

You may strive for this by convincing people of what you believe on an individual basis or by trying to create great works of art that move other people to see the world more like you do.

The core problem with this intrinsic value is it makes you resistant to new ideas. After all, if "you" are your current set of beliefs about the world and it is these beliefs you want to spread, you must also believe that the destruction or replacement of any of those beliefs involves some form of death, as by letting go of some ideas and accepting new ones, "you" will become less "you."

The hard question for this belief system is:
If, by pressing a button that would kill your body painfully and immediately, you could transfer 5% of what you believe about the world to every human alive, would you press that button?

You are the story others use to contextualize you within their lives

Within the formative days of Western culture, one of the most valuable things an individual could strive for was "kleos," which is basically glory as remembered in stories. Many still hold a similar belief: That the truest form of immortality is to have the story others tell about you last forever. This belief makes sense if you conceptualize the "self" not from an individual perspective, but from the perspective of others. This version holds that so long as the idea of us plays a role in the stories people tell, retell, and hold in their memories, we never really die.

From its earliest days, this belief was plagued with the obvious question: "Does it matter if you are remembered for having a positive or negative impact?" Consider individuals like Herostratus, a Greek arsonist who destroyed one of the Seven Wonders of the World just to preserve his name in the annals of history.

Even if you could be remembered in a favorable manner, is that enough? The hard question to ask yourself is:

Would you sacrifice your life for something that had near zero real impact on history, but left you remembered in a positive light for the next 500 years? (The charge of the light brigade for instance.)

Your Purpose

Some individuals believe that any entity acting out its purpose has objective value. With purpose being defined as what something was created to do.

An excellent demonstration of this concept is in the TV show *Rick and Morty* in which Rick, a mad scientist and inventor, is sitting at a dining table with his family and a robot he made to pass the butter.

Butter-passing robot: "What is my purpose?"

Rick: "You pass butter."

Butter-passing robot: (looking horrified down at its hands) "Oh my God."

Rick: "Yeah, welcome to the club."

Depending on how you contextualize what you are, your purpose may be so blindingly obvious and so simplistic that it is almost impossible to see as a thing of intrinsic value.

For example, if you are your body, your purpose is to procreate and maximize the spread of your genetic material. Your body and brain in a very real way exist for the purpose of spreading your genetic material within this worldview. Alternatively, if you are your current bundle of beliefs about the world and you think that a belief's purpose is to be spread, then spreading your beliefs is your purpose.

However, if you contextualize yourself as your mind or "mental substrate"—as opposed to the ideas your mind contains—you may conclude that your purpose as an entity is to test various ideas against each other.

It appears that a major evolutionary advantage in the human species is our ability to:

1. Make up various mental models or receive them from others (e.g., technology, lessons, or traditions passed down from generation to generation)
2. Test different mental models against each other
3. Discard faulty mental models without having to die

In other words, for spiders to "learn" how to spin better webs, the spiders that spin webs poorly must die, and the ones that make better webs will survive, reproduce, and thereby pass their genes. For a human to learn how to build a better house, he only needs to test various ideas against each other about how he may go about building a house and discard the inferior ideas. Our mental landscapes exist to allow ideas to compete.

If we view ourselves as our mental landscapes rather than our bodies or ideas, our "purpose" may be to optimize our minds to be the best possible battleground where ideas are tested and only the best survive.

If you contextualize yourself as your mind / mental substrate, ask yourself:
If you fulfill your purpose perfectly, but are neither remembered nor liked upon your death, have you lived a good life?

Considerations if you decide you believe your purpose has intrinsic value

While success metrics for someone who believes they are their body and their purpose is to spread their genes is fairly straightforward, it is harder to pin down exactly what "a good mental substrate for ideas" does on a day-to-day basis. If you seek to maximize the extent to which your mind weighs new ideas against each other and ensures the fittest ideas win, what should your long-term goals be? Is it important that you share those ideas with others? Could you move effectively towards your personal objective function by striving to ensure that other minds are working and processing ideas effectively, or must your mind process everything on its own to get "credit"?

To Have an Impact on History

When someone asks you on your deathbed what your life amounted to, there is an innate pull to want to be able to answer that your life mattered—that regardless of whether history remembers you, it mattered that you were born and existed.

From a logical perspective, this inclination comes from the assumption that an entity's value comes from how much it interacts with the flow of history and that an entity that does not interact with the flow of history does not matter. The hard question to ask oneself to determine if one really believes this is: If it is your interaction with history that imbues you with intrinsic value, would you sacrifice your life and the lives of all your relatives today—even if no one remembered you existed—so long as doing so guaranteed that you made a positive, lasting, novel impact on world history?

If you are not willing to make such a sacrifice and instead believe it is how history remembers you that matters, it is likely you are more inclined towards the objective function focused around attempting to obtain a type of immortality.

Considerations if you decide you believe that having an impact on world history has intrinsic value

Most who hold this intrinsic value believe that for it to be fulfilled, the impact one has on the world must be either positive or novel. They often also (incorrectly) conclude that the easier of those two features be ensuring their impact is novel. It is surprisingly difficult to leave a novel impact on world history.

There are few innovations one can develop, or feats one can achieve, that will not otherwise be achieved by someone else within a 50-year span. For example, most politicians outside of maybe a handful of world leaders are only surfing waves of sentiment. If these politicians had not become the public figures representing a particular zeitgeist to the world, approximately equal people would have taken their places.

This is even more difficult when you consider that most figures in world history that have had a novel impact have had a negative impact. It is much easier to be radically wrong than it is to be radically right.

It is therefore worth considering whether it matters if your influence on history is novel. If novelty matters, what can you achieve in your life that is novel? What can you do that will otherwise not be done this century?

Fairness/Equality

Many social primates have an instinctive inclination towards fairness. In one particularly vivid demonstration of this, scientists "paid" a Capuchin monkey to perform a task for cucumbers. The monkey was perfectly happy with its payment until it was exposed to another Capuchin who he saw was getting grapes for performing the same task. Upon seeing his colleague get better pay for equal work, this first monkey becomes clearly enraged.

Some people go so far as positing that our inclination towards fairness is more than a lower-order emotional pathway like lust and believe it to be imbued with intrinsic value, the typical argument being that if we feel a universal inclination toward fairness, it must have intrinsic value. While fairness is a relatively rare intrinsic value for someone to hold (typically, individuals only see fairness as an ideology for achieving distributed positive emotions), it is highly valued in modern Western society due to its utility in maintaining social order and its ability to signal virtue through social media platforms (virtue signaling—that is, showing off how virtuous one is—about fairness is uniquely unlikely to carry a social cost, while most other forms of virtue signaling can. Thus, fairness is used more often in virtue signaling due to its low social cost, which in turn increases its prevalence as a value within our culture).

If you believe fairness or equality to hold intrinsic value, questions you must ask yourself to test this belief should tease out whether you really just see fairness as a tool for distributing positive emotions, which would effectively make fairness an ideology (within the definitions used in this book), or whether you believe that fairness itself has value. The traditional hard question for this intrinsic belief is: Would you choose a society in which happiness and wealth are distributed equally, or a society in which everyone has more, but a few individuals have much, much more? A person who believes fairness has intrinsic value would prefer a society in which everyone had less happiness and wealth so long as what they had was equal.

Considerations if you decide you believe that fairness/equality has intrinsic value

It is much harder to define fairness than one may think.

Suppose a professor brings a cake to class and decides to split it fairly amongst the students of the class.[3] Does she:

- Split the cake into exactly equal pieces and distribute those?
- Give more cake to the hungrier students?
- Give more cake to the students who want the cake the most?
- Give more cake to the students who work the hardest?
- Give more cake to the students who come to class every day and exclude students who only showed up on that day hearing there would be cake?
- Give more cake to students from disadvantaged backgrounds?

---

[3] This thought experiment was inspired by one presented in *Policy Paradox: The Art of Political Decision Making* by Deborah Stone

- Not give any cake to the student who she saw murder an old lady with a rock?
- Give more cake to the students who would appreciate the cake the most?
- Give more cake to the students who would not be able to afford cake outside of class?
- Give more cake to male students because their daily caloric needs are higher on average?
- Give less cake to the students who bring a piece of cake to class every day?
- Give more cake to the nicest and most generous students?
- Give more cake to the students who have been having a bad week?

If you hold fairness/equality to be something of intrinsic value, the way you answer this question matters a lot to the way you choose to expend your one life in pursuit of fairness. Simple answers like, "to each according to their needs," often leave more room for interpretation than one may think.

Personal Improvement

People who believe personal improvement has intrinsic value define personal improvement in many ways, but generally argue that if you are a thing, there is intrinsic value in being the best possible version of that thing (be that "thing" the ultimate human, athlete, parent, salesperson, etc.).

The core difficulty with this intrinsic value is it lends itself very well to being a crutch to enable base addictions, whether the addiction be exercise, winning, or recognition.

The hard question to ask yourself about this belief is:
If you could be granted, with zero effort and maintenance, perfection at whatever aspect of yourself you are trying to improve, would you take it?

If you would refuse this offer, it is not the end state of perfection that you value, but rather the struggle for improvement (or perhaps you are just an addict trying to justify a thoughtless path in life).

If you agreed to the above offer for effortless perfection at whatever type of personal improvement you value, what would you do next? Why would that next thing be worth doing? Why is the next thing of less intrinsic value than improving yourself (e.g., why did you need to be perfect before dedicating yourself to this next task)?

If what you are trying to achieve is knowledge, change the question to:
At the press of a button, you can achieve perfect knowledge. The catch: you cannot disseminate it. Will you press the button?

If you would not press this button, ask yourself why it is important to disseminate knowledge. If you believe knowledge has value for its own sake, would you disseminate the knowledge if no one who received it could act on it?

Considerations if you decide you believe that personal improvement has intrinsic value

It is important to define two aspects of your goal if you chose this intrinsic value.

First, what specific aspects of your life have you chosen to perfect and why? When answering this question, it is useful to keep in mind all of the aspects of yourself you can work on perfecting, such as being perfect at your current job, being the perfect parent, or being the perfect friend/spouse/child/etc.

Second, are you striving for absolute perfection or relative perfection? In other words, do you want to be the best you can be or just better than others? Does the success of those around you in any way diminish your own accomplishments?

The Struggle

The struggle is the default intrinsic value for most with "Type A" personalities.

While almost nobody immediately concludes the struggle has intrinsic value, many arguments against other potential things of intrinsic value can lead people to believe the struggle for something, anything, imbues that thing with intrinsic value.

This realization comes when one recognizes that if one can get what one was striving for without work, it would lose all value—whether that be personal positive emotions or knowledge.

In this case, the intrinsic value of a thing increases the more you suffer to achieve it. An individual that believes this would say, "you must have intrinsic value relative to yourself and thus you can imbue other things with intrinsic value by sacrificing part of yourself for something else."

Still, this argument is a little flimsy, as it would only be arrived at by someone trying to justify their existing lifestyle rather than approaching the question of purpose a priori. Someone taking the a priori perspective would have stopped at existence having intrinsic value and would not have proceeded to create the additional special rule where you can imbue other things with value by sacrificing part of yourself.

Moreover, it is suspiciously convenient that humans are biologically susceptible to assigning higher value to more expensive things (for example, research shows a person will be happier owning a $5000 jacket than they would a $50 jacket even if they are the exact same jacket). Our susceptibility to this fallacy could be causing us to feel that things only have value if they are difficult to obtain.

It is important to recognize that even though "the struggle" can feel costly, a life of struggle can often be the path of least resistance. By losing ourselves in "the struggle," we can avoid having to think about why we are doing what we are doing and face the tough choices about what our life means to us.

This does not mean that "the struggle" lacks intrinsic value; it simply makes it a hazardous conclusion. If you decide "the struggle" has intrinsic value to you, please ensure that you are not just choosing it to avoid thinking.

Considerations if you decide you believe that the struggle has intrinsic value

Maximizing the struggle is difficult not just because it requires struggle. Is it worth throwing in pointless challenges to increase the difficulty of achieving a task? Does greater difficulty give any task greater value? Does the struggle still have value if it becomes routine?

Art and Inspiring Others

The argument typically used by those who dedicate their life to artistic endeavors is that there is intrinsic value in intellectually inspiring others. If this is your inclination, the first question you must ask yourself is: Did you choose to believe this to justify your lifestyle and self-image as an artist?

A good way to make this differentiation is to ask yourself:
Is it the inspiration of others or the creation of art itself that has intrinsic value?

If there is intrinsic value in inspiring others, then sharing a great book with two people who wouldn't have otherwise read it is twice as valuable as creating a great book that inspires one person. In this case, your time will almost always be better spent promoting great works as opposed to creating them yourself unless you are already a famous artist.

If you think the creation of art itself has intrinsic value regardless of the effects of the art on humans, ask yourself:
Is all art of equal value? Can the value of a piece of art be judged to be higher than the value of another if its effect on others does not matter?

If you hold that all art is of identical value, ask yourself:
Could you better maximize your objective function by quickly creating as many simple drawings as possible to increase the amount of "art" you produce?
If not, why not?

Considerations if you decide you believe inspiring others has intrinsic value

What exactly defines art? What kind of inspiration has value?

For example, does producing a critically acclaimed reality TV show satisfy your objective function better than creating one masterfully executed YouTube video with only a few hundred views?

Perhaps the most important question one has to answer when pursuing this path is what percent of your time and effort should be dedicated to *creating* your art and what percent is dedicated to *promoting* your art.

Experience Maximization

Some believe that intrinsic value lies in the diversity of one's experience. This means one's objective function should be to maximize novel stimuli through efforts ranging from travel to sexual experimentation or trying every type of drug one can in order to maximize the diversity conscious states one experiences.

The argument used to justify this intrinsic value is: What I experience has intrinsic value, but this value is not tied to the positivity of the emotions the experience leads me to feel. Instead, experiences have value based on their novelty. Even a positive experience loses all value as it becomes routine.

The hard question for this intrinsic value is:
Would you be willing to trade your life to experience the lives of every living human if doing so meant you would not be able to interact with the world while experiencing these lives?

Considerations if you decide you believe that experience maximization has intrinsic value

Maximizing experiences is an interesting objective function in that it is uniquely obtainable for almost anyone. Traveling the world can easily be done with even very low amounts of money by taking jobs for a year or so in each place one stops with the added benefit that these jobs can be quite diverse as well (if degrading and strenuous).

The most difficult aspect of this intrinsic value stems not from living in a way that maximizes it, but from overcoming the complacency inherent in the human condition that prevents us from even beginning to try something if doing so means defying social norms and venturing into new territory.

Protect and Promote the Growth of Human Civilization

Some conclude that the protection and development of human civilization has intrinsic value. This can result from one of three stances.

In the first two stances, either a person decides their purpose as a human being is to promote human interests, or a person sees himself as not an isolated entity, but rather a small part of a larger collective whole. Essentially such a person believes that they are just a small part of a larger entity, which represents the "real them." For example, if such a person were a blood cell in a guy named Carl and they were asked what they were, they would say, "I am Carl and what is good for Carl is good for me."

This argument can be thought of as similar to the argument for self-improvement, but instead of seeing yourself as primarily an isolated entity, you see yourself as a small part of a larger entity.

In the third case, someone believes humanity is imbued by intrinsic value through some particular trait (typically the complexity of our culture and the intelligence of the members within it).

You can differentiate individuals who believe that human civilization has absolute rather than relative intrinsic value by asking:

- By what metric does human civilization have intrinsic value when contrasted with other primate cultures (like those observed in chimpanzees)?
- If an alien species with more of that characteristic wanted to remove humans from the planet and replace them with aliens, should I not assist the aliens in this task?

If you believe that human civilization has relative intrinsic value, you should have no problem saying you would instead fight to protect humanity, but should you believe, humans have absolute intrinsic value based on some set of human accomplishments, you would be obligated to fight on behalf of the invading species. The "hard question" for individuals who have the more common relative perspective is:

Would you kill yourself today if it moved human civilization forward technologically and culturally one year?

Considerations if you decide you believe that protecting and promoting the growth of human civilization has intrinsic value

What exactly does growth mean in this context? How can you dedicate your life and resources to best move humanity in a "forward" direction?

To a large extent, this answer is mediated by the probability you see of humanity being wiped out in the near future. Even if you see a threat as having a 1% chance of wiping out our species in the next half century or so, it would be logical to dedicate your life to neutralizing that threat.

If you think instead that there are no real threats to the survival of our species, you must then decide whether to spend effort on technological or social progress. If you spend time on social progress, how do you determine what positive social progress is? If "positive social progress" is making other people feel good, should your objective function not be to maximize positive distributed emotions?

Accumulation of Knowledge as a Species

Some conclude that there is inherent value in accumulating and distributing knowledge about the nature of the universe.

Typically, this is tied to a belief that as conscious entities, we can only increase our own intrinsic values through the spread of information. Difficult questions to ask yourself to determine if you really hold this value are:

Would you sacrifice yourself to add some bit of knowledge to the human dataset if (1) that knowledge would not have otherwise been added but (2) it is of no practical value?

-And-

If you could press a button and it would give all humans absolute knowledge, would you press it?

Nature and Biodiversity

There is something viscerally upsetting to the collective Western consciousness about the destruction of large swaths of habitat and species. While some individuals frame the upsetting nature of this destruction as being related to some other intrinsic value ("Think of all the medicine that might not be made now that we lost the rare plants from which it might be derived!"), others believe nature has intrinsic value in and of itself.

These individuals typically place value on biodiversity specifically. They fight significantly harder to protect endangered populations in contrast to common species.

The most difficult challenge for any individual who believes that biodiversity has intrinsic value is that the very visceral assumptions that lead us to hold these beliefs do not lead us down the logical path to actually maximize biodiversity.

If all life holds value, the continuation of life is of intrinsic value, and our goal is to maximize biodiversity—then shouldn't we be putting our effort into seeding other planets with anything we can get to grow on them in an effort to create new, lush biomes?

Even if this path of seeding other planets with life only has a fraction of a percent probability of working, the potential upside of a biome as lush and diverse as earth is so much greater than the upside of almost any conceivable conservation effort on planet earth itself that such efforts are trivialized.

You may argue that the biome in which our species evolved has a higher relative value to us than any biome on another planet, but in this argument is the admission that our biome only has value because it is the biome in which humans exist, which most people who hold this intrinsic value would find disconcerting.

Considerations if you decide you believe that nature and biodiversity have intrinsic value

What is the best way to maximize biodiversity in the universe?

Even if you believe that existing species within our own biome have some unique value, is your time not always better spent trying to protect small insects and plants that require less support and can be maintained more easily? Is there value in developing methods to catalog the genetic material in our world so it can be recreated later if future humans decide it still has value?

The Continuation of the Universe

For some, existence itself is a thing of intrinsic value and perhaps logically the thing of ultimate intrinsic value. After all, if all the deeds you perform in your life are ultimately futile in the face of the heat death of the universe (the mainstream belief in physics that the universe is expanding at an increasingly rapid speed and will eventually be so spread out that atoms will almost never interact with each other, being miles apart).

This view logically leads an individual to dedicate one's life to somehow preventing the heat death of the universe, as without external intervention, the heat death of the universe is both inevitable and the single most inherently negative thing that could happen.

Within our lifetime this dedication typically takes the form of preventing the early death of our species and advancing physics and technology in general as fast as possible. In future ages in which we have a better understanding of physics, this intrinsic value may lead to radically different behavior.

The hard question one can ask oneself to determine if one really believes existence has intrinsic value is:
What if we learn that we can "reset" the universe (and that it has been reset before), but we can only do it sometime in the next ten years? Would you pull the trigger to make that reset happen and erase all of human civilization?

Considerations if you decide you believe that the continuation of the universe has intrinsic value

This intrinsic value is unique in that it may not be physically possible. It may turn out that the universe ending in heat death (or some other way) is a categorical imperative of physics.

Assuming that it is possible to avoid the heat death of the universe, there are many questions still left open about what is required to maximize this value. Let us explore four potential scenarios for you to decide at which point the action has intrinsic value:

1. We can split off a new universe from our own, but the laws of physics in it are different in such a way that life will never come to exist in it.
2. We can split off a new universe from our own but are not able to transfer any information about our universe into it.
3. We can split off a new universe from our own and are able to transfer information into it.
4. We can split off a new universe from our own and are able to move a colony of our own species to it.

Some also argue that we are inside a simulation that would render this whole intrinsic value moot (reportedly Elon Musk is a big fan of this argument). The argument goes: If a simulation complex enough to model human society is possible to build, it is likely that hundreds if not thousands of them will be built at some point. If thousands of such simulations will be built, it is more likely we are living in one than not.

However, if you believe this objective function and conclude that we cannot know whether we are in a simulation, it is your moral imperative to assume we are not, as whatever a simulated person does is irrelevant anyway, and you know for a fact there is a chance you are not in a simulation.

Maximizing Lucidity / Enlightenment

The belief that lucidity (or enlightenment) has intrinsic value surfaces in several religious traditions as well as numerous new-age philosophical movements. Those who believe lucidity has inherent value make it their objective function to maximize the amount of time they, and others, spend lucid (that is to say: not on autopilot, tending to their various worldly and bodily distractions). This is often attempted through regular and prolonged meditation, mindfulness, and/or prayer.

When not derived through a religious dogma, this belief is sometimes arrived at by an individual who initially believed maximizing the time they were alive had intrinsic value, but ultimately decides that different states of consciousness have different levels of intrinsic value. If you were to spend your entire life on autopilot just reacting to stimuli, your life, per this objective function, would have no intrinsic value.

The hard question for those who believe that lucidity is a thing of intrinsic value is: Would you live the rest of your existence in a tube unable to interact with the world or feel happiness if doing so maximized your ability to maintain full control over your consciousness?

Considerations if you decide you believe that maximizing lucidity has intrinsic value

The vast majority of those who dedicate a large portion of their lives to maximizing lucidity do not pursue lucidity because they believe it has intrinsic value. Instead, such individuals have an ideology (a hypothesis about how the world works) that maximizing lucidity gives them access to some form of supernatural power whether this power be a closeness to God or the ability to influence their reincarnation. These people should focus less on lucidity and more on their ultimate objective function.

However, if you genuinely believe that the lucidity itself is your goal there are a number of interesting nuances to clarify. Are moments of lucidity still valuable to you if your resulting reflections on the world are wrong? What if your lucidity-generated conclusions are correct, but based on bad information? For example, Deepak Chopra has almost certainly spent more time reflecting on life than you, but he also has a poor understanding of even basic theoretical physics and neuroscience. Has Deepak Chopra lived a life of more intrinsic value than yours?

If you decide you believe that moments of lucidity that lead to a fundamentally incorrect actions, revelations, or views about what action you should take are less valuable than moments of lucidity that lead to correct conclusions, what about great thinkers of the past who based their now obviously-wrong conclusions on the science of the time? Did they live lives of less value than someone maximizing lucidity today? Since future individuals will almost certainly view us the same way, would your life not strictly be better spent advancing human science, so you can increase your (or our species' collective) ability to reflect intelligently on life?

Value Uncertainty

Value uncertainty comes from the belief that something has intrinsic value, but either you do not know what it is yet or you believe it is impossible to ever truly determine what has intrinsic value. While there are far fewer flavors of value uncertainty than there are flavors of independent values, value uncertainty represents a much more common way of viewing the world. We will quickly detail a few objective functions that can arise from being uncertain about what holds inherent value.

The Search

Some individuals see value uncertainty as simply a stage in their development towards discovering what has intrinsic value. These individuals are in the process of searching for what they believe is true about the world. Essentially, these individuals build their objective function around building a better objective function.

Having had at least one phase in your life in which you are in the process of "the search" is extremely helpful later. Likewise, it is healthy to always have some aspect of the search built into your objective function, no matter how confident you may be that you found something of intrinsic value. Having had a period of complete dedication to this mindset may make you more receptive to new, better, potentially objective function-changing information should it arise.

Covering Your Bases

An individual selecting this objective function attempts to maximize as many things of likely intrinsic value as they can. This typically manifests itself as an individual dedicating their objective function toward pushing forward technological progress, as this benefits almost every likely objective of intrinsic value.

It is easy to underplay the benefits of technology but consider that today even someone in the bottom 30% of the U.S. population lives a significantly better life than kings did just a few centuries ago (not living in constant pain, getting to eat a wide variety of non-spoiled food most of the year, varied and high-quality entertainment on demand, etc.).

Essentially, such a person says: I don't know what has value, but if I attempt to maximize all potential things of value simultaneously, I will probably get something right.

Focus on What Society Says is Good

While defaulting to what society says is good is a common objective function for people who are uncertain about what holds objective value, this is one of the few objective functions that is patently wrong. An individual who defaults to this objective function trusts social consensus over logical, reasonable thought.

Keep in mind that society has many other reasons to frame ideas as "good" outside of the best interest of the individuals who make up that society. For example, bad ideas may be framed as being good in the name of social cohesion or the benefit of a powerful ruling class or "intellectual" elite. In addition, some ideas spread very easily on social media regardless of how sound the logic behind them is, as they can be used to virtue signal (such as those ideas involved in politically correct culture). This results in such ideas being more commonly held in modern society than ideas that cannot be used to virtue signal.

Focus on Personal Proclivities

In this case, people default to focusing on whatever they have a personal proclivity towards (typically personal happiness) with the assumption that if they cannot determine with certainty exactly what has intrinsic value, it is not worth pursuing anything.

Religious Intrinsic Values

The goal of this guide is **not** to talk anyone out of a religion.

We are in a difficult position, as the first step of our framework is to clarify your objective function and determine why you have chosen that objective function by questioning and clarifying your core beliefs. However, there is a deep cultural sensitivity towards a religious individual being asked to question and justify their beliefs. Moreover, there is a deep sensitivity for a non-clergy member to discuss the implications of objective functions derived from religious beliefs. For these reasons, we will keep our discussion of religiously derived objective functions relatively generic, with a focus on those most common in U.S. culture. We will nevertheless ask you to honestly question your beliefs.

When a steel sword is made, it is repeatedly heated until soft, then quenched in a cold liquid. This process is called tempering. Blades are tempered to increase the toughness, impact resistance, and elasticity of the metal while decreasing its brittleness, a trait it gains by being overly rigid. By heating your beliefs through honest questioning—by genuinely considering you may be wrong—then quenching the beliefs in a world that will make their truth self-evident, you remove their brittleness and make them even tougher.

If you do not allow your faith to be tested with novel lines of questioning, it may atrophy and become weak, brittle, and unable to respond to genuine threats. Thus, when addressing challenges to your belief system, it is best to avoid the natural tendency to immediately dismiss them, thinking to yourself: "This person is wrong, and I just need to explain how." Instead, ask yourself: "Is this person wrong, or am I wrong?"

A person who becomes defensive or angry when asked to strengthen their beliefs by questioning them is someone with an underlying fear that if they questioned their beliefs, they may abandon them. Such people have only superficial faith.

We encourage you to approach challenges to your belief system from an unbiased perspective and use logic and an imaginary opponent's perspective to come to a well-considered, consistent, and compelling conclusion. In addition to strengthening your faith, this approach can make you more effective at sharing your religious views.

Religious beliefs in this guide are divided into four categories: Hard Belief Systems, Soft Belief Systems, Personal Belief Systems, and Self-Image-Based Belief Systems.

Hard Religious Belief Systems

This guide defines a hard belief system as any religious belief system that strongly adheres to a cohesive religious tradition. Almost all these belief systems have been refined by thousands of great minds over the ages, resulting in a large cohesive body of interconnected beliefs about the world that are represented by religious traditions like Southern Baptism, Mahayana Buddhism, Sunni Islam, and Orthodox Judaism.

The most important question anyone with a strong belief system must ask themselves is: Why do I adhere to my particular belief system and none of the other similar (but mutually exclusive) systems that exist?

This question becomes uniquely poignant when you just happen to believe the religion into which you were born or the predominant religion within your local culture. It would be a remarkable coincidence that the religious tradition prominent in your community at the time of your birth just so happens to be the one correct tradition.

When developing your argument as to why you believe your particular religious tradition as opposed to another, it is important that you not rely on arguments that a party arguing from the opposite perspective could also use in good faith.

Imagine you are asking a Christian why they are a Christian and not a Muslim. This Christian may say: "I am a Christian and not a Muslim because when I ask God in my prayers, He tells me that I chose correctly."

This is not a very strong argument, as millions of Muslims around the world would use the exact same argument when explaining why they are not Christian. They would believe this argument just as strongly as this Christian. When they pray and ask God what they should believe, He tells them to be Muslim.

This Christian also cannot use the argument that countries that are predominantly Christian are more technologically advanced, stable, and treat minorities and women "better." While this may arguably be true today, it is undebatable that for parts of the Middle Ages, the Islamic world was both technologically and culturally more progressive.

Were this Christian to adhere to this line of reasoning, they are arguing that, had they had been born in the Middle Ages, they would have been Muslim, which they obviously believe to be the wrong religion. Therefore, condemning the current culture in regions where various religions are predominant is not an effective method for judging the inherent truth of a belief system.

This Christian could argue that they know Christianity is the correct system because Jesus either was closer to God than Muhammad or that Jesus performed more miracles than Muhammad. However, if they rely on this argument, they are tacitly accepting that if someone on earth today started performing better miracles than Jesus and also claimed to be God, they will dismiss the Bible in favor of this new person's teachings.

Alternatively, this Christian could argue they are Christian either because Christianity fulfilled a prophecy provided in earlier religious teachings or that Christian prophecy has been historically predictive of future events. However, in each of these cases, Muslims can claim the same thing: that Muhammad was prophesied in the New Testament and that the Koran has predicted future events.

Anyone justifying their faith with either of these criteria tacitly admits that if an even more predictive historical text were to be found, they would choose it over the Bible as a source of truth, or, should a person in our time fulfill the prophecies in an old religious text more perfectly than Jesus, they would accept this person as a higher source of authority (if that is what those older texts predicted they would be). Such an individual would also need some metric for quantifying the unique predictive capacity of their chosen religious tradition and would need to study other religious traditions' predictions to ensure they don't "out prophesize" them based on said metric.

In other words, a person cannot claim their religion is uniquely predictive if they haven't studied the veracity of predictions in other religions or criticisms of the claimed predictions within their own religion.

In addition to knowing why you believe your religious tradition is more correct than vastly different traditions, you should also know why your tradition is the correct one when contrasted with more similar traditions. It is easy to avoid thinking through this topic and say, "I believe what is in my religious text," but remember that for almost every mainstream religious tradition, there are multiple sects with significantly different views of the world that would all make the same claim. Calvinists, Quakers, Puritans, and Baptists, for example, would all claim that they simply believe what is in the Bible, yet they come to very different conclusions.

If you take the hard religious tradition path in life, it is crucial to ensure you are following the correct tradition. Truth isn't a team sport. Examining related-yet-different sects is not about finding ways to argue that the sect in which you grew up (or is popular in your community) is correct; it is about using the cognitive abilities a higher power gave you to come as close to the truth as possible. You must take time to understand the different ways people throughout history have interpreted the text you know is true, so you can come to the truest possible interpretation of it. Getting this question correct is quite literally the single most important thing you will ever do.

As with other aspects of applied pragmatic thought, it is a shame that our current society provides no good unbiased resources to help you make this determination. Any religious authority figure or community has a vested interest in delivering information to you in a way that guides you toward their sect's interpretation of religious scripture—not out of malice, but because after years of meditating on the topic, they obviously believe their particular sect is correct, just as hundreds of thousands of equally intelligent and well-meaning scholars of the same texts have come to different conclusions.

While this book doesn't have the space to delineate how all of the world's various religious sects differentiate themselves and explain the philosophical, interpretational, and historic (often political) reasons for those differences, this book can guide you as you perform this exploration yourself. Given that most readers of this book who follow a hard religious path will follow one of the Abrahamic religions (due to the language in which it is published and the geography in which it is distributed), we will use them as a model.

On our website (Pragmatist.Guide/Religion-Tree [or if you can copy and paste, http://pragmatist.guide/Religion-Tree/]) is a tree that can serve as a very rough map for exploring how the different sects of the Abrahamic religions relate to each other. It would be impossible to create a 100% accurate map; the map provided is only meant to serve as a rough reference point. The best way to use this map is to start at the base branch that contains the last human (or entity on earth) that you believe shared divinely inspired teaching and then begin to work your way forward, tracing how various groups interpreted those teachings.

As you work your way along the tree, perform research to understand why the people of each sect had a different interpretation of the teachings than you do. Think through what specific historical factors may have led them to misinterpret the meaning behind specific aspects of your religious tradition and note similarities between those historical factors and ones that may have influenced the genesis of your own tradition. It is natural to have a blind spot to missteps in our own belief systems, but by spotting missteps in similar but related traditions, we can better mark areas of our own belief system that require more careful scrutiny.

This investigation will not be an easy or quick task, but if it gets you closer to truth, it is patently worth your effort. Sometimes this task may be as simple as clarifying why you believe the canon of religious texts you follow to be correct (such as coming to an understanding of why the Gnostic Gospels are dismissed by modern Christians and the more mainstream canon is accepted).

This task may be as complicated as parsing out elements of truth from a historical political or power struggle within a religious organization that resulted in different sects that ultimately interpret the same texts quite differently. You may find yourself agreeing with elements of each interpretation when you dig into the logic behind these differences. In other instances, you may be delighted to find a small element to truth in an interpretation of the religious texts that is no longer common for reasons other than the truth of said interpretation (such as the difficulty proselytizing the predestination of the Calvinists or the celibacy of the Shakers).

Do not be tempted to formulate arguments that make it easy to end on the branch of the tree that dominates your local culture and social groups. You are seeking the truth, not arguments that allow you to maintain the status quo.

Just as anyone with a strong belief system needs to have a good reason for knowing why they are a member of their tradition as opposed to any of the other traditions, someone who subscribes to a strong belief system should be clear about what that belief system says has intrinsic value, what their objective function should be, and what ideologies (hypothesis for maximizing those values) the tradition supports.

In a similar vein, keep in mind that while a hard religious belief system *may* inform your objective function, it does not *always* spell it out. For example, it may not be clear just from religious texts how important converting people to your faith is when contrasted with acting in a way your deity would approve of or contributing to make the spiritual lives of those already faithful richer. Would you carry out an unethical action if it helped you convert someone and benefit them for eternity? Having a clear understanding of your objective function in the context of your faith is still an important task.

Soft Religious Belief Systems

This guide defines soft belief systems as any religious belief system that loosely adheres to a cohesive religious tradition. Often soft belief systems take a religious tradition and alter it to make it better conform to mainstream social trends.

Soft belief systems are defined by statements like: "I am Jewish, but I believe that all religions are different ways of looking at the same truth" and "I am Christian, but I believe you go to Heaven no matter what you believe so long as you are a good person."

While there are many logical reasons to gravitate towards softer interpretations of mainstream traditions, soft belief systems run the risk of being forms of self-image-based belief systems in which you allow your self-image to define what you believe about the world (e.g., I am a good person, a good person wouldn't believe that their nice, gay, and Hindu friends are going to Hell; therefore, my religion doesn't say my friends are going to Hell).

Additionally, an individual with a soft belief system should reflect on whether what he believes is simply the path of least resistance in life allowing him to believe that he is going to Heaven (or whatever reward their tradition offers) without having to make any major costly changes to his daily behavior or how he interacts with people of other faiths.

The core question you must be able to answer if you hold a soft belief system is:

Why are some aspects of the tradition true while others are false? More specifically: what logic or common characteristic allows you to toss out certain parts of a religious tradition?

You should be uniquely suspicious of a common characteristic if it relies on a modern western interpretation of morality, as it would be a remarkable coincidence if you just happen to be born into the culture with the correct interpretation of morality. Consider that what is moral has varied widely throughout history as is evidenced by the fact that you even feel your religion needs a "morality update," as said religion was obviously considered moral within the time and culture it was created.

Personal Religious Belief Systems

Personal belief systems are at least in theory not heavily influenced by any religious tradition. In these belief systems, through some logical argument, you have built your own beliefs about the nature of the supernatural world and what it wants from you. The most common belief system in this category (in the Western world) is some form of Deism; therefore, we will focus on questions related to Deism below.

Due to the fact that Deism is not a mainstream belief system within our culture, most individuals who are Deists have put some thought into their beliefs about God, as they had to turn away from another tradition to become Deist, and therefore it is difficult to bring up a challenge to their belief system that they would not have seriously thought about already, but that is still generic/broad enough to have a place within this guide.

If you identify as a Deist, think through what evidence you have that the deity is not perfectly evil instead of perfectly good.

Almost all evidence typically used to prove that God is good could also be used to prove God is evil. For example, you could argue that God created the pleasant things in life so that bad things in life would hurt more (as opposed to arguing that God created the bad things in life to increase the value of the positive things).

Additionally, the many different mutually exclusive revelations of God that have followers who, when they pray to God, believe He tells them they are following the right path seems to be direct evidence for a God that is lying to at least one group (assuming you see supernatural signs and communication as evidence of God). Would a perfectly evil God not reveal himself in slightly different mutually exclusive ways across regions to increase the amount of conflict and hatred in the world?

Again, you could argue that it is in the nature of an all-powerful deity to be perfectly good, but there is no apparent form of this argument that could not be twisted to say that it is in the nature of an all-powerful deity to be perfectly evil. Some would counter this argument by saying evil is just the absence of good, so such an entity couldn't be maximally evil, but again, such an argument could easily be twisted to say good is just the absence of evil, hence a maximally powerful entity would have to be maximally evil.

Finally, you could just argue that God defines what is good—therefore, whatever He does must be good, but this feels like a hollow argument. Being a good entity has no value if anything you do gets defined as good.

If you end up deciding that God does exist, but that he is a maximally evil entity, or that you cannot be certain if He is good or evil, then your objective function would change significantly. (Like everything else in this guide, this is just a thought experiment meant to challenge a person's belief system. We are not actually arguing that God exists and that he is evil.)

As with every potential belief system, we encourage you to clarify exactly what your personal belief system states is right and wrong and make clear conclusions about what that belief system dictates you should maximize with your life. To determine this, look towards whatever source of evidence you viewed to be strong enough to justify building your own supernatural belief system.

Personalized Hard Religious Systems

While unusual, these religious systems are extremely interesting to contemplate. In such systems, a person believes everything contained in a certain religious dogma is true except for the implications that the dogma claims those things imply.

For example, someone may that believe the Bible or Quran is a 100% accurate record but based on that record conclude that God is a petty, malevolent entity. Such a person may even believe God is being honest when He says He loves all humans, but that God's love is more like the love of an abusive partner who threatens to torture you if you don't love him back. Such conclusions might lead someone to come up with fascinatingly unique objective functions.

Such belief systems are rare to the point of essentially not existing within most Western religious traditions but are increasingly common among the Eastern tree of religions as interpreted by Westerners. For example, one could believe everything taught in traditional schools of Buddhism is accurate but conclude that Siddhārtha Gautama was wrong in his assessment that ending the cycle of suffering and rebirth was the correct aim based on that information. Such an individual may disagree with the assessment that the suffering caused by attachment is more intrinsically negative than the positive emotional state they are able to experience. Alternately, someone may disagree that suffering is inherent to the human condition, and if suffering is not an inherent part of life, the four noble truths are not truths. With these lines of thinking, some rather exotic objective functions (exploiting the concept of reincarnation) might arise.

A person who holds one of these unique interpretations of a hard religious system must be able to explain how no major group in history ever came to hold such beliefs when they had access to the exact same information. The major religions have been systematically obsessed over by the greatest minds in human history, and yet they did not come to the conclusions you did. Why? What knowledge, perspective, or information could you possibly have access to that they lacked?

Self-Image-Based Belief Systems

Our first instinct when thinking through belief systems is to first decide what "type of person" we are and then "choose" whatever belief system that "type of person" would believe. When this train of logic is approached with even the slightest amount of incredulity, it reveals itself as patently wrong and destructive.

Some belief systems are primarily driven by the way an individual wants to think about himself and not by any sort of logical pathway or tradition. Essentially an individual first decides a bunch of generic positive things about themselves such as: "I am a good, powerful, counter-cultural, spiritual, person" and then designs or shops for a belief system that allows them to best maintain these beliefs about themselves.

These belief systems are best personified in the perpetual archetype of the high school Wiccan or the Evil Eye Chuunibyou[4], but are also common in

---

[4] This is a Japanese term sometimes used interchangeably with "eighth-grader syndrome." It is used to describe early teens who, through a desperate desire to stand out, have convinced themselves that they have hidden knowledge or secret powers. While this is a normal part of growing up, it is important not to build a lasting religious perspective around it.

many new age belief systems. Obviously, an individual would never admit to themselves why they hold these beliefs while they still hold them, but enough of us have passed through these phases ourselves to recognize the pattern.

It is not worth expending effort trying to tease out the logic behind these types of belief structures, as by definition they are not based on logic. If these belief systems were logical, they would fall into one of the other categories.

Almost any belief system can fall into this category if arrived at by asking: "What kind of belief system would someone like *me* choose?" For example, if someone were a nihilist because he identifies with the goth subculture, then their nihilism should be categorized as a self-image-based belief system instead of genuine nihilism.

This is the only belief system category we will openly condemn (however, we like to think we can retain the claim of being unbiased, as this is not a condemnation of any specific belief system. Any belief system can be arrived at from a non-self-image-based perspective). We advocate (1) determining what you believe is true about the world and (2) leveraging those beliefs to develop your self-image. Self-image-derived belief systems follow the exact opposite order: (1) determining how you want to see yourself and (2) shopping for a belief system that validates that self-image.

Essentially, when choosing your core beliefs about the world (whether they incorporate a religious tradition), it is crucial to remember that you are not shopping for the pre-packaged framework that best fits your personality, existing lifestyle, or desired public image. **You are searching for what you think is most likely to be true.**

Proclivities

There is a very good chance that you will unconsciously work something devoid of intrinsic value into your objective function. You will consciously know this thing has no intrinsic value, but you may *still* work it into your objective function. Non-intrinsic values that work their way into your objective function are what we call proclivities.

We work proclivities into our objective functions because we know we will be unable to take the sometimes hard-to-swallow "pill" of our objective functions without adding a sweetener to it. You may be a famous musician who has logically concluded that all humans' emotional states are of equal value and given the vast amount of poverty in the world, if you followed your "raw objective function," you would have to give away almost everything you owned. Realistically, though, you may also realize that you could never get yourself to accept or stick to this. To get yourself to accept your objective function, you may need to add in factors like a personal happiness threshold that must be met before you are willing to help others (you get to keep your house, cars, exotic shark collection, and fame, but everything beyond that goes to the poor).

We ask individuals to include their proclivities in their objective functions because if they do not do so, they make up false ideologies to protect themselves from truly challenging their beliefs and making the sacrifices necessary to achieve what is truly meaningful to them.

Those subconsciously trying to justify proclivities may convince themselves that they would be less effective at redistributing their wealth if they lived in a one-room house instead of their mansion. Never make the habit of lying to yourself like this. Recognize your weakness of character and accept it. Hopefully in the future, you will become a better person and shed more of your proclivities.

Common proclivities include:

- Fame
- Comfort
- Happiness
- Conformity
- Honor
- Sexual gratification
- Being remembered after death

- Minimizing the suffering of those around us

Proclivities sometimes resemble intrinsic values. One person's intrinsic value might be another person's proclivity.

For example, personal happiness may be of intrinsic value to Edward and minimizing the suffering of others may be of intrinsic value to Xiang. At the same time, Edward might have a proclivity for minimizing others' suffering, and Xiang might have a proclivity for personal happiness. Nevertheless, if Edward or Xiang focused on their proclivities instead of their core intrinsic values, they would do a poor job at achieving their objective functions, as their proclivities merely distract them from what really matters.

We want to believe that our proclivities have wormed their way into our value systems for a good reason: "I am more productive when I am happy," you might say to yourself. "I can't work hard on things that have real value without a base level of happiness." Sometimes these statements are true, but often they are lies, and at best, most belong as ideologies—hypotheses about how to achieve an objective function, such as "I hypothesize that happiness makes people more productive."

The important thing to remember is this: When you must choose between a proclivity and your objective function, your objective function takes priority. For example, if feeling comfortable and dignified is a proclivity you have, but to achieve something related to your objective function you must become uncomfortable and lose your dignity for a while, you should not waver in your choice to endure those discomforts.

Regardless of their real value to us, proclivities are part of being human. The most we can expect from ourselves is to be cognizant of what is a real intrinsic value and what is a proclivity when optimizing our lives.

Step 1 Wrap Up

If this is your first time systematically thinking through what you believe about the world, you have been given a huge amount of information to process. We recommend setting aside specific periods of time in your day to mull through it all—such as while you are taking a shower or when you are about to fall asleep. Better yet, if you are reading this book with a friend or a group, take some time to discuss these ideas with them, perhaps while on a walk or in some other circumstances in which you have a clear head.

After thinking through specifically what you think has (and/or does not have) intrinsic value in the world and identifying your personal proclivities, define your objective function. An objective function can be structured however you want it to be, for example: "after achieving a specific happiness threshold, I want to dedicate my life to maximizing the speed of technological development." Whenever you must make a decision in life, whether it be your choice of college, spouse, pastimes, or friends, reference your objective function and the decision will often become obvious.

While you only have one objective function, that function may have many components. These components can include multiple proclivities and the maximization of multiple things you believe to have intrinsic value. Each of these various components should contain a modifier that describes how it will relate to the other components. This modifier can be anything from a threshold (I have to have X amount of happiness before I focus on other elements of my objective function) to a percent (I will dedicate X% of my time resources and income to distributing happiness and Y% to maximizing personal lucidity). Once you have built your objective function, you will have an easy reference for the efficacy of any decision you make on achieving your objective function in life.

Step 2: Develop Your Ideological Tree

If Jane's objective function is to please God, she might have ideologies that include human equality, Southern Baptism, Democracy, Monogamy, American-Style Democracy, and the Republican Party. While each of these ideologies represents a hypothesis about how to achieve the same objective function (e.g., pleasing God), they are not equal in importance.

Some of our ideologies are directly subordinate to others. Jane's pro-life ideology is directly subordinate to her ideology that delineates when life begins, which is directly subordinate to her religious ideology. Altering an ideology lower in one's ideological tree affects all the ideologies above it. Were Jane to change her ideology about what counts as a living thing, she may have to revisit her views on abortion.

Your beliefs about the world can be visualized as a tree in which a few senior ideologies inform thousands of subordinate ideologies. Even minor shifts in our understanding of senior ideologies (that is, ideologies near the trunk of the tree) affect the rest of our worldview. We should, therefore, spend significantly more time refining our most fundamental ideologies, even though we naturally dread the process of doing so, as changes we make to them send shock waves throughout all branches of our ideological trees.

Ideologies and Objective Functions

Ideologies are not tied to specific objective functions. One person's objective function may be another person's ideology.

Consider the case of freedom. One person may believe freedom itself has intrinsic value (and thus build their objective function around it) while another person may have an objective function built around maximizing distributed positive emotions but believe that promoting freedom is the best way to boost general happiness.

Having a solid picture of your ideological tree enables you to interact intentionally and logically with the world. Unlike objective functions, which are ultimately judgment calls, ideologies can be proven categorically wrong. It is possible to unequivocally prove that a certain ideology is not the best way to maximize an objective function.

Standards for Evidence

Before you can approach and prune your ideological tree to ensure it properly serves your objective function(s), you must first establish what information you will consider as evidence. What may be compelling evidence to one person could be ridiculous conjecture to another, so two people with the same lives and experiences may come to build very different ideological trees based on their standards of evidence alone.

Sam has an objective function oriented around minimizing human suffering. Sam may read in a well-respected newspaper that most scientists believe global warming is a very serious threat. Should Sam think information from well-respected newspapers counts as evidence, he may integrate climate change mitigation into his ideological tree. Clarissa, on the other hand, may read the exact same article and have the exact same objective function, but not integrate climate change mitigation into her ideological tree if she does not consider news articles claiming most scientists agree on something as a viable source of evidence.

To be an actualized, effective individual, you must consciously decide what information warrants the creation of new hypotheses about how the world works. This threshold will be your "standard for evidence."

What evidence do you need to alter a deeply held belief? What would it take, for example, to make you believe—or not believe—in ghosts?

If you do not believe in ghosts, would personally seeing a ghost convince you, or would you assume you were going crazy or suffering from carbon monoxide poisoning? Would you believe in ghosts if five people in your close family claim to have interacted with them? Would a detailed report in the New York Times indicating that most scientists now believe ghosts exist convince you even if you never personally saw one? Would you have to read peer-reviewed, scientific studies in reputable journals concluding the existence of ghosts before changing your mind?

If you do believe in ghosts, what level and type of evidence would be required to convince you that you are wrong?

It is extremely dangerous to hold beliefs that will not change regardless of the type or strength of evidence presented.

Because changing our minds is such a difficult task, decide ahead of time what type and level of evidence is necessary for you to update your beliefs. If you wait to encounter evidence before deciding what level and kind of evidence is enough to warrant change, your natural tendency to resist change will allow you to manipulate your standards in the moment to avoid having to change your beliefs (some people call this "moving goalposts").

There are seven types of evidence that (almost) every human uses to update their theories about how the world works:

1. Logical Consistency
2. Personal Experience
3. Personal Emotional Experience
4. Cultural Consensus
5. Expert Consensus
6. Scientific Method
7. Doctrine

We will discuss each of these types of evidence in turn.

Consider which types of evidence trump others for you. When your personal experiences contradict expert opinion on a subject, which version of reality do you internalize as true? The hierarchy of evidence you create is entirely within your control (and a personal judgment call—there is no clear right or wrong). That said, all humans are naturally drawn to some standards of evidence over others.

We will call the standard of evidence you hold that dominates over all other standards of evidence your "primary standard of evidence." Though the hierarchy of standards you personally set will significantly influence how you perceive reality, the primary standard you select will make the biggest difference. It is nevertheless possible for lower-ranking standards to "gang up" on your primary standard if evidence is copious enough. This can be seen among individuals who suffer from paranoid schizophrenia—they almost always succumb to believing some aspect of their hallucinations, even if they are entirely logical people, because after personally experiencing something vividly and frequently enough, it becomes difficult to ignore that information, no matter how much it violates one's primary standard of evidence.

Standards for Evidence Explored in Detail

Logical Consistency

Logical consistency is by far the most common primary standard for evidence. Outside of individuals who establish personal emotional experience as their base, if someone told us they had any other primary standard of evidence, we would assume they mean "after logical consistency of course."

It is very rare for obvious logical inconsistencies to appear in our beliefs about the world (that is, beliefs held by the type of person who would read this book), as most mainstream beliefs about the way the world works are already logically consistent and any inconsistencies that do arise are explained away by individuals who we believe are smarter than us and have far more free time. To find a commonly held logical inconsistency, you would need to delve into conspiracy theories.

A good case study for looking at logical inconsistency is the belief that the moon landing was faked. Consider the following three points that most people believe:
A. The Soviet Union and the United States where genuine enemies during the cold war,
B. the Soviet Union was not so completely incompetent as to not notice we faked the moon landings, and
C. the Soviet Union did not claim the moon landings were faked.

If you believe these three points, the standard of logical consistency would trump even compelling evidence that the moon landing was faked.

Though all our minds strive for logical consistency, we almost never use this standard to overturn existing ideologies—even if we really value logic. It is one thing to admit to yourself you were wrong about something because you didn't have all the facts, but quite something else to admit you were wrong about something due to a logical inconsistency that self-reflection could have uncovered. For this reason, even among individuals who would swear that logical inconsistency trumps all other forms of evidence, logical consistency is almost never evoked to update their beliefs.

Personal Experience

An individual who establishes personal experience as their primary standard for evidence would override any set of current beliefs based on a personal experience. While many of us assume this is our ultimate standard of evidence ("I'll believe it when I see it"), it is in fact a relatively rare standard to maintain at the top of one's hierarchy.

Suppose a voice speaks to you, tells you it is the voice of God, and asks you to join the Church of Latter-day Saints. Do you do it? An individual who places Catholic Doctrine as their primary standard of evidence would dismiss this as a trick of the devil, whereas someone who holds expert consensus (in this case the consensus of the scientific community) at the core of his standards of evidence may experience this and dismiss the experience as a psychotic episode and become concerned that he is developing schizophrenia.

If you are one of the rare individuals who would respond to the above event by unquestioningly becoming a Mormon, personal experience may therefore be your ultimate standard for evidence. Knowing what you would do if a voice, claiming to be God, spoke to you and said something that did not align with your existing religious beliefs is valuable in understanding the true nature of those beliefs.

While personal experience is extremely rare as a primary standard of evidence, personal experiences may be so powerful that they override higher standards of evidence in your hierarchy. For example, suppose you heard the voice of God telling you to join the Church of Latter-day Saints not just once, but every morning for five years. While at first you may dismiss the voice as schizophrenia, after five years you would likely believe it—even if you have just as much reason to believe it is still schizophrenia.

Personal Emotional Experience (Gut Feel / Intuition)

Someone who establishes personal emotional experience as their primary standard for evidence will believe something is true because it "feels" true to them (whether they have personally perceived it within their lives). These people often describe themselves as "going with their guts" and making decisions based on "intuition."

This is the most "natural" of all the primary standards of evidence in that it is the standard all humans default to when they cannot muster the emotional control required to suppress it. It is not a great personal failing if you feel drawn to believe something because it "feels right" even though you logically know it is a poor standard of evidence. This compulsion is a sensation all humans know (or at least all humans who try to overcome their base instincts).

Personal emotional experience is the primary standard of evidence used by a large portion of the population. It is particularly common amongst spiritualists, practitioners of new age philosophies, and individuals who have certain soft religious beliefs (e.g., "I believe everything in the Bible except for anything that is inconvenient and makes me feel bad").

This standard for evidence is unique in that it is the only primary standard for evidence that does not require logical consistency. The ideological trees of individuals whose hypotheses about the world are predicated on whether something feels right (or is pleasant, interesting, comforting, or otherwise emotionally easy) are riddled with inconsistencies.

For example, individuals who establish a religious doctrine as their ultimate standard of evidence will still find it a valuable exercise to explain how apparent contradictions in their religious texts are only superficial misinterpretations. An individual who relies on personal emotional experience would not be concerned by such contradictions as long their conclusion feels right to them.

Because our emotional experiences are not bound to a logical framework, individuals who "go with their guts" make for uniquely frustrating debate partners for those who use other standards of evidence. While one may be able to convince an individual using gut feeling as their standard of evidence that there is no logical way the principle behind homeopathy is accurate (i.e., that diluting a substance does not, in fact, increase its potency), this will not influence his belief in homeopathy so long as it *feels* true to them.

Individuals relying on emotional experiences as their standard of evidence often find it equally frustrating to convince those who prioritize other standards of evidence, defaulting to arguments designed to attack one's emotional attachment to a concept. Such a person may argue against a scientific or religious concept by labeling it as racist without internalizing that people with other standards for evidence do not use perceived racism as a barometer for truth.

Intuition does not always run against logic. It is well documented that human intuition works well for repetitive tasks so long as one has experience with them and the tasks involve immediate positive or negative feedback. Outside of these very narrow situations in which intuition is effective, it is equally well recorded that intuition does *not* lead to "factually correct" decision making (despite what some poorly researched pop science books claim). That said, it is relatively irrelevant whether a thing is "factually correct" to a person who makes decisions based on their emotional experience, as such a person believes that factual correctness is a lower order of correctness than emotional correctness (something feeling true).

Cultural Consensus

An individual who establishes cultural consensus as their primary standard of evidence will dismiss all other standards of evidence—whether they be something they personally experience or something their religious text clearly states—should that evidence go against the norms of the subculture with which they identify.

Cultural consensus as a standard of evidence almost never refers to the consensus of society as a whole, but instead the consensus of one's personal subculture. If one's subculture—such as a religious community—has another standard of evidence as its cultural norm—such as religious doctrine—one may appear to be following this other standard of evidence (instead of what they are *actually* doing, which is deferring to the consensus of the subculture with which they identify).

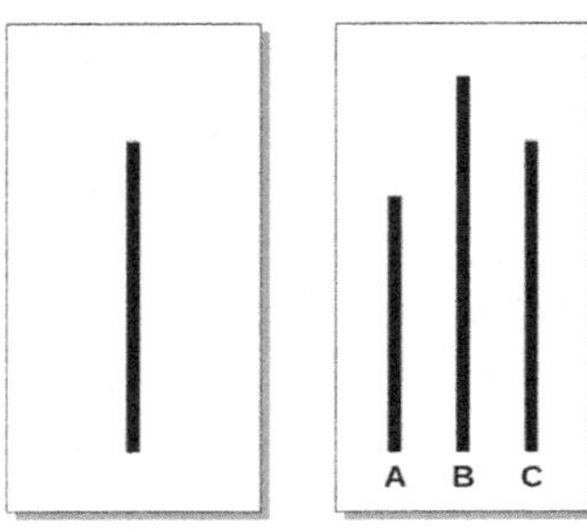

[5]

This standard of evidence is almost as much of a human default as personal emotional experience. Study after study has shown that people will trust "the group" over their own personal experiences. The Asch conformity experiments go so far as to show that when everyone in a room is saying the line on the left is the same length as line B, only 25% of people ignore the consensus in favor of what their senses are telling them. Among the 75% of participants who are influenced to follow the group, follow up studies demonstrate that some perceived what the group was saying as being literally true

---

[5] Image by Fred the Oyster, CC BY-SA 4.0-3.0-2.5-2.0-1.0, via Wikimedia Commons

and saw the line as being the same length as line B because they heard a number of other people say it was. [1]

This standard of evidence has become the predominant standard of evidence within large swaths of the academic community (something that can come as quite the shock to individuals who have never worked in academia). For example, well over half of 335 social psychologists responding to a study conducted by Buss and Von Hippel reported that if their research—or that of a colleague—found a biological basis for sex differences, the findings should be obfuscated.[6] These finding demonstrate a particular subculture's belief that the equality of all humans should take precedence over any scientific evidence to the contrary. (One of this book's sequels, *The Pragmatist's Guide to Sexuality*, explores how subcultures within politics within academia have twisted the mainstream interpretation of sexuality into something that does not align with the data).

None of this should come as a surprise. Humans are social animals, with brains designed for social conformity. Consensus with one's personal subculture is by far the most common primary

---

[6] See: "Psychological Barriers to Evolutionary Psychology: Ideological Bias and Coalitional Adaptations" in Archives of Scientific Psychology

standard of evidence amongst the general population.

Expert Consensus

An individual who holds expert consensus as their primary standard of evidence is willing to disregard even deeply held beliefs if an educated, expert community (as they have defined it) deems them inaccurate. Individuals who hold expert consensus as their primary standard of evidence may turn to consensus among physicists for information on how the fabric of the universe works, turn to the heads of the religious community for information on what will get them sent to hell, and turn to a respected newspaper for information on what is happening in the Middle East.

Two people who rely on expert consensus may have very different ideological trees depending on who they consider to be "experts" on different subjects. For example, consider the issue of autism and vaccines. Some people consider the medical community to be experts, and therefore do not believe that vaccines cause autism. Others consider online researchers to be experts, and therefore believe that vaccines cause autism.

Even those referring to the same expert community can come away with very different beliefs depending on their thresholds for consensus. One individual may update his beliefs based on a single well-conducted study published in what he deems to be a respectable peer-reviewed science journal whereas another may wait until thought leaders in a particular field update their beliefs.

Ironically, it is almost impossible for a great scientist or thought leader to establish expert consensus as his primary standard of evidence. To truly become great, a scientist or thought leader must be able to vastly alter mainstream conceptions in a field based on personal experiences. This individual may have to believe for years or decades that almost every other expert in his field is fundamentally wrong about how their field works.

An archetypical example of this would be Charles Darwin, who, drawing from his personal experiences in the Galapagos, essentially rewrote everything that was previously accepted about biology. If Darwin had genuinely held contemporary scientific consensus as his standard of evidence, he would have dismissed any personal experiences that conflicted with that consensus. Therefore, many individuals who hold expert consensus as their primary standard of evidence make an exception for fields in which they consider themselves to be experts.

Scientific Method

A person who holds this standard of evidence will disregard the consensus of the scientific community if they believe the body of research produced by that community does not align with the expert consensus in the community. For example, if such a person encountered an extremely well designed and executed study with a huge sample size come to a conclusion that is radically different from the scientific community's present consensus, such a person would alter their viewpoint on the topic before the community itself did.

This is an extremely rare standard of evidence to realistically execute on: It requires regularly consuming vast amounts of information, developing a deep understanding of what constitutes a well conducted experiment in a large number of different fields, and a knowledge of the experiments around which the community has built its present consensus (because no matter how good an experiment is, such a person would only change their view if that experiment presents better data than the sum of all data from all other experiments conducted on the subject).

This standard of evidence is more dangerous than most would assume. It is common for individuals who hold it to not invest the time necessary to truly understand why the scientific community sides with the existing body of evidence over a random study this person found online or in an obscure journal. Studies that get shared a lot are not more likely to be true; there are just more likely to be counter intuitive, salacious, or otherwise shocking. This is why communities that hold this standard of evidence so often end up performing bizarre practices, such as eating sticks of butter every morning after reading one study that suggests it will be healthy. If you are not able to constantly monitor all major work being released in a field or do not have a robust understanding of experimental design, we would recommend you just default to expert consensus over conclusions drawn from specific studies.

I (Malcolm) would see such a primary standard of evidence as being completely unfeasible for a real person to maintain in a responsible way (who is not a practicing scientist in a field) if I did not know that the other author (Simone) regularly reviews every major cognitive psychology study released then adds anything she finds pertinent to her worldview to a master document she maintains as well as a note on the strength of the experimental design. If you are not a practicing scientist making judgment calls within your field, maintaining this standard of evidence with any fidelity will require at least reading every major study in a field on a weekly basis.

I should note my views on this subject have changed considerably since we first published this book. In one of our subsequent books, The Pragmatist's Guide to Sexuality, we dug deep into just how much politics have affected the current academic consensus. This has disillusioned me to the point where I now make a point of funding my own studies to sanity check parts of the academic consensus that are likely to be politically motivated. The results of these personally funded studies have led me to lose faith that the consensus within a few domains of social science is based on an analysis of data and thus I more aggressively distrust other domains I have yet to personally research.

Doctrine

An individual who accepts doctrine as their primary standard of evidence allows evidence from a selection of written works (or cultural history) to trump all other forms of evidence. Though religious doctrine is the most common source material, political ideologies are sometimes used as well, particularly in communist and fascist countries.

An individual who establishes a doctrine as their standard of evidence almost by necessity does not have a "reason" for following their doctrine, as the doctrine itself is the highest order of truth. Because of this, such individuals often have a difficult time persuading others to their way of thinking due to a tendency to rely on arguments like: "This book is the word of God; you can see right here in the book—it says that this is the word of God, so your book is not."

Such arguments are only persuasive to an individual already using that particular text as their standard of evidence.

While doctrine, particularly religious doctrine, may seem common as a primary standard of evidence, it is in fact fairly rare. The primary standard of evidence for most religious individuals is cultural consensus within their religious subculture or expert consensus among their clergy—not religious doctrine.

An archetypical example of expert consensus and religious doctrine clashing can be seen during one of the lines of argument during the Protestant Reformation, in which some Christians began to argue that the beliefs of the experts within their religious community were not in line with the religious text.

These thinkers framed the core schism between Protestants and Catholics as a disagreement about which standard of evidence people should use, specifically: Is something true because it is in the Bible, or is something true because the highest-ranking individuals within the religious community generally agree it is true? Essentially, can an average person come to a better understanding of the Bible by reading it themselves, or by asking someone who spent their entire life studying it and thinking about it?

Like these early Protestant thinkers, almost any individual who follows religious doctrine as a standard of evidence will be seen as an iconoclast (even within their own religious community) because the mainstream culture of any religious community strays from its core tenants over time. Religious communities deviate from their doctrine with time, as individuals who value personal self-interest over doctrinal fidelity inevitably gain power within communities. Such people have the ability to represent a religion as something more palatable or profitable (giving them more marketing dollars) than its true doctrine would. After all, the church that tells you your friends aren't going to hell is usually going to outcompete the uncompromising church amongst all but the truest of believers.

An individual who sets religious doctrine as their standard of evidence will ironically not find a comfortable home among most practitioners of their religion, as the way they will approach their religion will inevitably force them into conflict with the majority of the religion's practitioners who are instead following a cultural consensus. This confrontation is a threat to the power structures within an established religion, hence individuals who take doctrine as their primary standard of evidence are typically publicly shamed as extremists to decrease their influence.

The most used primary standard of evidence amongst those who identify as religious—cultural consensus—is an objectively bad primary standard to use. However, it is less obvious whether using doctrine or expert consensus as one's primary standard is a superior approach for the average believer.

As discussed above, some religious traditions even regard expert consensus as superior to doctrine. This is typically found in any religious tradition with a single governing body and allows for such traditions to update their beliefs by decree, like the Church of Latter-day Saints updating its views on polygamy or the Catholic church updating its views on evolution. However, even outside of the kinds of religious traditions that hold councils of experts to update their beliefs, holding expert consensus as a standard of evidence greater than doctrine should not be interpreted as making an individual "a bad believer."

Many people, perhaps correctly, lack the confidence to believe that they have the training and the intellect to notice something in the texts of their doctrine that centuries of experts did not.

Building the Base of your Ideological Tree

Having been presented with the concept of an ideological tree, you may feel compelled to map your ideological tree in its entirety. Given the plethora of potential ideologies addressing nearly every aspect of life, fully mapping out your ideological tree is virtually impossible and not an effective use of your time. It is nevertheless helpful to map out the base of your tree.

The base of your ideological tree and the hierarchy of your core ideologies are important to think through, as these higher-order ideologies (at the tree's base) will influence all your lower-order ideologies (in the smallest, farthest twigs).

Once you identify the ideologies at the base of your ideological tree, challenge them. Questioning ideologies close to the base of our trees requires monumental effort, so we are less likely to change these hypotheses over the course of our normal lives—even when we are presented with compelling evidence suggesting they are inferior or wrong. Instead, we interpret efforts to share such evidence with us as direct attacks on our personal identities and become too defensive to really think through whether our ideologies match the evidence to which we currently have access.

If you react angrily when a certain core ideology of yours is attacked, that ideology deserves special attention and extra scrutiny. Focus on ideologies that create a visceral feeling of disgust (fringe political ideologies for example). Don't fall into the trap of telling yourself: "I don't believe X because people who believe it have Y wrong with them." Instead, scrutinize the ideology itself. Try to view it from a fresh perspective.

Most importantly, for all of your most core ideologies, consider what new evidence you would need in order to change your opinion. If you believe capitalism is the best economic system to support your objective function, what evidence would you need in order to change your mind and conclude that communism is preferable? Have you ever tried to find that evidence? It is remarkable how rare it is for us to seek out evidence suggesting our core beliefs about the world could be wrong, despite how beneficial such evidence would be. After all, if you are wrong about something important to you, would you not want to know?

Ideological Trees Require Regular Pruning

Throughout our lives, we will gain access to new information that may disprove or alter our perspective of a particular ideology. As we alter senior ideologies within our ideological tree, we need to remember to review subordinate ideologies after the alterations are made to maintain consistency across the tree.

For example, suppose you are considering a polyamorous relationship and had previously assumed that monogamy was your preferred relationship model. In such a scenario, rather than merely asking yourself: "Should I be polyamorous now?" you should ask yourself:

- What made me think monogamy was the best way to approach relationships given my objective function?
- What information made me think I should consider polyamory instead?
- How does this affect the rest of my beliefs about relationships?

Ideologies that Require Careful Scrutiny

One of the strongest innate drives in the human mind is an addiction to not thinking and a tendency to choose the path of least resistance (as opposed to the option that will assist us in achieving our objective function).

Because of this, there are two categories of ideologies you should scrutinize more than others:

- **Any mainstream or near universal ideology within your culture, especially one that is "improper" to question.** Good examples of ideologies to question under this rule within modern Western society might be the virtue of equality, the sanctity of human life, or the inherent wrongness of eugenics. These are all ideologies that almost everyone you interact with on a daily basis agrees with and that the questioning of is a massive social taboo; therefore, they are likely the ideologies to which you have applied the least critical thought. It is easy to argue that if everyone seems to agree on something, it is not worth thinking about. However, remember that societies change their concept of morality over time. There is no guarantee that the future will treat our current society any kinder than our current society treats the slaveholding South.
- **Any ideology that discourages critical thought.** A good common example of this is the ideology that encourages the lifestyle of "just going with the flow and listening to your emotions" alongside "don't think too hard about things." Many cults and certain religious traditions also fall into this category, insisting that there are paths of logic you are not allowed to even consider and thoughts that are evil to have.

Leveraging Social Interaction to Better Think Through Your Ideology

Thinking through an ideological tree is not something that can be done in one sitting or by yourself. One of the best ways to build and fortify your ideological tree while challenging the baggage you accumulated by chance involves talking it through with someone else who is willing to question basic beliefs and assumptions (including their own). Close friends can be excellent for these conversations, though due to strong cultural taboos against these sorts of topics (with the classic adage that religion, sex, politics, or money are not topics of polite conversation), it can be difficult and has the potential of jeopardizing a friendship.

Step 3: Define Your Internal Character

Disclaimer (totally skippable)

All previous chapters of this book focus on information that is objectively true and are meant to be as unbiased as possible. The intent of this chapter holds to that precedent: After you decide what you want from life and how you plan to achieve it, it is objectively worth reflecting on, designing, and becoming the kind of person that would be best at executing your plan. However, the question of how to change oneself requires some hypotheses on how humans think, which removes us from the realm of objectively true and unbiased statements.

First, we must assume a position on what standard of evidence we reference when looking for information on this subject. Given its wide acceptance within our culture, we have chosen scientific consensus as the standard of evidence when possible. When we lack scientific consensus, we default to information gained from personal experience and conjecture based on research. To us, this seemed the most "pragmatic" solution to a situation in which we are forced to take a stance on standards of evidence and ideologies.

We have to rely heavily on limited research and findings from personal experimentation throughout this chapter, as there is no universally accepted model for how the human brain processes emotion at a systems level. While, from the perspective of a neuroscientist, we can say the right precuneus (along with at least a dozen other regions) plays a role in happiness, that information does nothing to help the reader understand how people think.

Even well-trodden, evidence-based models designed for behavioral change, such as cognitive behavior therapy and dialectical behavioral therapy, are focused more on changing problematic responses to stimuli and less on gaining a holistic understanding of how to sharpen a healthy mind into a more powerful tool. That is not to say psychologists have not begun working on these questions under the title of "positive psychology." However, the field is new enough (and infested with enough pseudo-science gurus) that we are unwilling to hang our hats on any claims it makes as being "scientific consensus." Positive psychology is still in the transition phase from pop-science to real science, having only been first pushed for in 1998.

Because of this, we have had to build an easy-to-understand, quickly explainable, "close to accurate" model of how a normal, healthy person processes and responds to their experiences on a day to day basis. This easily accessible model should allow anyone to train themselves to alter undesirable personal traits and shave the rough edges off their personality to create the most optimal version of themselves. That said, we need to stress that the model described in this chapter is not the "whole truth" of how emotions are processed, which will be elaborated on later in this section. Nevertheless, we will have an easier time improving ourselves if we use a simple model and not a more nuanced understanding of the admittedly messy human brain.

This model for how we process experiences is a product of personal experience, cognitive behavioral therapy theory, neuroscience, research on neural networks, evolutionary psychology, and marketing. While the model draws heavily from mainstream schools of thought on cognitive behavioral therapy, it does deviate in some small ways by incorporating inspiration from other fields.

For example, cognitive behavioral therapy (CBT) argues that our emotional reactions to situations are primarily based on learned schema about how the world works, whereas the model described in this chapter is based on the theory that our emotional reactions are derived by our unconsciously referencing a personal mental model similar to the mental models we use to predict behavior in others. This alteration is proposed based on inspiration from these other fields:

- ***Marketing**: Businesses sell to consumers by convincing them they need something to maintain a certain perception of themselves, not by priming schema (unless those schemas are tied to sex).*
- ***Evolutionary psychology**: It appears that higher cognition first evolved amongst humans for the purpose of modeling people and behaviors, not for the sake of storing information in an organized library of rulebooks.*
- ***Neural networks**: Referencing the already-existing "mental model" system we use to predict behavior in others would be a "cheaper" way for the brain to process emotional reactions (in comparison to cross-referencing a separate library of schema).*
- ***Schizophrenia research**: It appears that Schizophrenia is at least in part the result of the mind having overactive mental models, which come to be interpreted as external stimuli (voices in one's head); because this overtaxing of the mental model system*

appears to affect emotional responses, it would suggest the systems are linked.

While this chapter's different approach may seem superficial, it is at least worth flagging. We have no consensus model of human behavior on which we can base this section, so we have had to develop and test our own. Obviously, if you prefer the cognitive behavioral therapy model of emotions, we encourage you to research cognitive behavioral therapy further.

So far, this guide has focused on the topic of how people would think and live their lives in an ideal world: How people determine what they believe about the world, decide what they want from life based on those beliefs, develop hypotheses about how to best achieve those goals, and then execute on those hypotheses. Unfortunately, as we are humans and not hyper-rational robots, this is not a realistic way to live life on a daily basis.

It would be nearly impossible to constantly reference your goals and beliefs about the world every time you make a split-second choice or decide what you will say next in a conversation. Doing so would require immense mental processing power.

Instead, most choices humans make about how to interact with the world are made unconsciously on "autopilot." While there isn't a scientific consensus on exactly how this autopilot works, it is clear that this autopilot is neither static nor beyond our influence. Instead, it appears that we have an internal model of ourselves that represents what kind of person we think we are, and we unconsciously reference that model to determine how to react in various situations. This model appears to work similarly to the mental models we use to predict others' behavior. This mental model system is likely the same system you are utilizing when you have an imaginary conversation with someone else in your head.

To put it simply, when you are practicing an argument with someone in your head, you have sectioned off a part of your consciousness and assigned it a "mental model" imbued with characteristics you think the person you are arguing against would hold. The "program" in your head that controls your reactions to someone in real-time conversations is essentially the same mental model program, only it is imbued with characteristics you believe describe you.

Thus, when you experience potentially reaction-inducing stimuli, such as an insult, you do not think, "To further my goals, what is the best way for me to react to this insult?" but rather subconsciously ask, "How does someone like me emotionally, verbally, and physically respond to being insulted like this?" Depending on the type of person you see yourself to be, this can lead to reactions that you know run contrary to your best interest.

This unconscious response only creates an initial impulse to respond in a certain way. That impulse can be overridden by the logical parts of our conscious minds. This is done through inhibitory control mechanisms in the ventromedial and dorsolateral prefrontal cortex. Unfortunately, these inhibitory mechanisms can be weakened by a number of factors that prevent you from controlling your initial impulse.

Factors that limit your ability to exercise inhibition include:

- Alcoholic intoxication (widely known to influence inhibition)
- Lack of sleep, which prevents your brain from functioning at full capacity (inhibition is very cognitively taxing)
- Lack of myelination in the dorsolateral prefrontal cortex (this region doesn't fully myelinate until your late teens, leading to inhibition being more difficult for younger individuals)
- Dedication of the inhibitory sections of your brain to other tasks (such as fighting a desire to smoke, stay on a diet, or ogle an attractive person)
- Fatigue from recent inhibition (numerous studies have shown that the inhibitory sections of our brain can be exhausted if used frequently over a short period of time)

Ideally, we should strive to have an unconscious mind that creates initial impulses that we need to inhibit as little as possible. We want our internal model of ourselves to be so closely aligned with the type of person we desire to be that our initial impulse is what we would choose to do if we had the luxury to carefully consider and choose reactions that best serve our objective functions. Fortunately, you can change this initial impulse by changing the type of person your unconscious mind sees yourself to be—by changing the "model" of you that it is using for reference.

Learning to change the internal model your unconscious mind uses to determine your reactions to stimuli does more than give you control over the initial impulses you have—it changes the emotions you feel. In other words, by changing your internal sense of self, which determines how you react to things, you can change your emotions.

Consider how not everyone feels anger when they are provoked. Only those who feel justified in feeling anger when they are provoked, given how they see themselves, will feel anger. If your unconscious doesn't see yourself as the kind of person who gets angry when provoked, you will not feel anger when provoked. Feelings like anger, sadness, and envy occur because your unconscious mind feels it would be appropriate to indulge in that emotion given what it understands about your place in the world.

How to Turn Off Autopilot and Create Your Identity

Even the most self-aware person lives most of their life on autopilot. We decide to take vacations because we see ourselves as the type of person who would take that trip instead of asking how a vacation will benefit our personal goals. We post things to social media sites because we see these things as the sort of content someone like us would post—instead of asking how it benefits us to post that thing.

Some individuals don't ever leave autopilot. Many even decide what they believe about the world while on autopilot instead of thinking through what they actually believe is true (e.g., "I am a good, deep, spiritual person—what do people like that believe?").

Below, we will discuss both how to turn off your autopilot and how to create an autopilot that generates impulses you don't have to inhibit because they represent the way you would want to act were you not on autopilot.

Leveraging Moments of Lucidity

Almost everyone will see value in learning to occasionally break through the haze of autopilot and create brief moments of lucidity, during which one is capable of thinking: "Is this really what I believe is the right thing to do?" and "Does this really serve my goals?"

While it is easy to create moments of lucidity in which your autopilot is off, it is trivial in the same way getting out of bed on a day when you have nothing to do is trivial. You might lie in bed thinking, "You know, I should really get out of bed," but there is another part of your brain that pleads, "But why? This is working for us right now; just go with it"—and that other part of your brain often wins.

It becomes easier to silence those parts of our brain if we have moments of lucidity built into our weekly schedule. These "periods of audit," in which we have time set aside to evaluate all of the major decisions we have made that week, can ensure our actions aligned with our goals and beliefs about right/wrong. Just as with exercise, these periods of audit are easier when we build them into our daily routine and easier still if we manufacture social pressures that encourage us to stick to those routines. For example, you may schedule a morning walk and talk with your significant other during which you discuss your goals for that day and that week, how you plan to further those goals through concrete action, and what major decisions you have coming up in your life.

While it may become easy to create moments of lucidity with practice, creating a mental state in which we can rewrite our internal models—the personal blueprints that determine our autopilot—is extremely difficult. While in a moment of lucidity you may think: "It is not helpful for me to react angrily in a situation like the one I encountered yesterday. I should really not do that in the future," merely having that realization will do little to change your behavior or your internal model of self. Instead, to be able to rewrite your internal model, you will need to put forward a considerable, sustained effort during a period of flux.

Leveraging Flux Periods

Flux periods are times in our lives during which we can rewrite and adjust our core mental models. Periods of flux are not states that we can consciously create, they are turns of events that happen to us. That said, we can trick our brains into entering them.

As long as your life is static, you will be extremely limited in your ability to rewrite the personal mental model that governs your unconscious behavior. However, when our lives are not static, it is as if the code that makes up our personalities becomes malleable. During these periods, our internal models of self will almost certainly change, whether we choose to change them, they serendipitously change, or our environment/social group influences them.

These periods of flux—moments in which your internal model can be edited—can occur during:

- **Major life transitions:** Many people experience a personality reinvention between high school and college, when moving to a new city for a new job, when getting out of prison, etc.
- **Major social transitions:** If you are transitioning social groups (especially if your schedule also significantly changes), it is possible to enter a period of flux—even if you are not in a novel environment.
- **Moments experiencing abnormally high levels of oxytocin release:** This happens when one is falling in love, dating a new person, etc.
- **Hitting rock bottom:** This may involve entering prison, nearing the end of an addiction spiral, nearly dying, losing everything in a divorce, etc.
- **Getting high:** Altered states of consciousness achieved through meditation or drugs, particularly certain hallucinogens, can lead an individual into a state in which one can rewrite their self-model. Unfortunately, while these altered states of consciousness allow us to rewrite who we are and what we believe, they enable us to make these changes during a time in which our cognition is impaired. New beliefs and personalities born from such states may be inherently defective when contrasted with those born of sound minds. (Do you really want to make one of the most important decisions in your life in a cognitively impaired state?)

It is easy to read the above list and through reflecting on your own life realize that your personality did change some during periods like those described, and you had no idea just how susceptible your personality was to being rewritten during such periods.

To drive home how malleable your core internal programing becomes during periods of flux like those described above, consider that when heroin addicted soldiers returned from Vietnam, the massive shift in social and environmental conditions allowed 95% of them to shake their addictions. It is unlikely that you have any personality trait more deeply written into your unconscious than an addiction to heroin.

Obviously, we won't always have the luxury of being in the midst of a major life transition. Because of this, we should mark these flux periods as they appear on the horizons of our lives and specifically take note of what we want to change about ourselves during these brief windows of time. If, however, you see no potential flux periods on the horizon and you wish to update yourself in the near future, you can attempt to create a period of flux artificially.

Artificial flux periods can be created through one of two methods: the sabbatical and the localized reboot.

In the sabbatical method, an individual creates a short-term major change in their life, schedule, and environment. This may involve living in another country for a couple months while focusing on updating your internal model. However, this method is unrealistic for most due to limited finances, limited vacation days, and regionally locked jobs. Changes made during these sabbaticals might also fail to stick if you return to a completely unchanged home, schedule, job, and social set after the sabbatical finishes.

The localized reboot involves moving to a new neighborhood and building completely new routines, surroundings, and social networks. Obviously, this is not easy to do either, but so long as your life remains static, rewriting who you are as a person will be incredibly difficult.

Revelations

A revelation is a phenomenon that occurs when an individual changes a significant part of their ideological tree during a flux period. Revelations make changing your internal model nearly effortless and allow for vast changes in character. The downside of revelations is that the new ideologies which prompt them will become defining characteristics of your identity (and internal model) going forward.

Examples of people changing their internal models through revelations include a person experiencing a "finding Jesus" moment after hitting rock-bottom, a freshman in college deciding that communism is the best form of government, or a teenager discovering "The Red Pill" after being dumped by his first long-term girlfriend.

Unless you have a hard religious objective function, we recommend that you avoid allowing revelations to "write your new identity," as they can lead to dogmatic beliefs in whatever aspect of your ideological tree you changed. However, revelations are fantastic tools for those following a hard religious path, as dogmatic obedience towards specific ideologies can beneficially augment the execution of their objective functions.

To illicit a hard religious revelation, use a period of flux to focus a significant portion of your free time on the exercise discussed in the "hard religious" objective function section of this book, which is designed to help you clarify your religious beliefs. Once you gain access to some new way of seeing your faith, you should focus on what that says about the type of person you should be.

An Autopilot-Altering Case Study

I, Simone, had an objective function that involved having a large family, however I suffered from fertility issues. I felt so much stress and anguish around these problems that it began to interfere with my work and health and lead me to lose focus and sleep (making it even less likely that I would overcome my fertility issues).

By talking this situation through with Malcolm, I realized that I felt this way because I saw myself as a Type-A perfectionist—someone who beats herself up about any and all failures. I decided to question whether beating myself up about failures helped me achieve my objectives in life. "Does fear of personal mental punishment motivate me?" I wondered.

In a moment of clarity, I realized that my habit of being hard on myself did *not* motivate me to work harder. If anything, my type-A personality was demotivational, as it kept me in a negative mindset.

Knowing that I would be starting at grad school in the near future, I made a note of my type-A personality as something I wanted to alter about myself when I rebuilt my internal model within the new social context of grad school. Once in my period of flux, I kept a diary every day in which I wrote from the perspective of the new person I wanted to be.

I was ultimately able to remove the negative emotions associated with my situation by recontextualizing myself as someone who does not punish myself for failures outside of my control. My saddened state lifted, I slept better, my focus improved, I found all sorts of tasks easier to tackle, and, ultimately, I was able to build a healthy and happy family.

Arguments Against Choosing a Self-Image

Choosing what makes us happy, sad, angry, and envious is a choice available to everyone, but a choice very few of us decide to make. As with anything in life that requires self-reflection, we instinctively reach for flimsy excuses allowing us to avoid responsibility for our own lives.

When being reminded that you can choose who you are and that you are responsible for any failure to live up to your own ideals, your natural response will be to shirk that responsibility.

To avoid improving themselves, people often grab for the following shields:

- "I am who I am. I can't change myself."

- "I would no longer be 'me' if I change my internal self-image."
- "Emotions are natural. I trust them to steer me in the right direction."

While it is patently false that people don't change, there is some merit to the idea that we essentially "kill" parts of ourselves by changing our internal models. If we contextualize ourselves as whatever views and ideas we hold RIGHT NOW, we are absolutely destroying parts of ourselves by changing our self-images. This is nevertheless largely irrelevant, as if you do not choose to change yourself, the world will change you. Parts of you will inevitably die. The only question is whether those parts of you will die by your hand, or that of serendipity + time.

It is also worth asking yourself: "Is a version of me that was created by external pressures a truer version than a version of me that I consciously designed?" If you see your identity as a sticky ball, would you rather it be covered with whatever dirt it picked up rolling down the road, or would you rather wash it off and decorate it with whatever you want?

We would argue that a "you" that you independently and consciously design is more genuine than a "you" someone else (or mere chance) created, but ultimately this is a personal judgment call.

With regard to emotionally driven decisions: history makes it clear that emotions do *not* always steer people in the right direction. Nearly every war crime, genocide, and rape has been committed by a person acting upon an emotion. Emotions do not somehow magically lead us down the right path; they do not even assist in their own maximization (i.e., if your objective function is to maximize positive emotional states, it would be worth rewriting your internal model into one that is not as affected by whatever gets you down most on a day-to-day basis).

If you believe in evolution, like us, you will also likely believe that emotions exist only because our ancestors who had them had more surviving offspring. Thus, there would be no reason to believe that emotions have special access to "truth" or "genuineness." If you do not believe in evolution, you will see that almost all religious frameworks warn about the dangers of outsourcing higher cognition to base emotions. For example, in the Christian framework, emotions are the primary tool the Devil uses to lead people away from God. Even if the only thing in life you believe has purpose is the maximization of your own positive emotions, you will *still* be better off if you logically manipulate your emotions.

Finally, not mastering your emotional state can literally shave years off your life. Extended periods of anxiety, irritation, or depression can lead to problems with blood pressure and your heart. Positive emotions have even been shown to enhance the immune system while negative emotions suppress it, leading less happy people to get sick more often.

What Builds Our Self-Images if We Do Not?

Five outside forces build our internal models when we do not take personal responsibility for their development: social conformity, cognitive dissonance, personal ego, reinforcement, and instruction.

By looking at how the internal models of ourselves are changed by outside forces (rather than ourselves), the triviality of these characters becomes more apparent.

Social Conformity

The slow grind towards conformity to a peer group can shape your internal model. This causes you to develop the self-image of someone conforming to your peer group, but different in some trivial, inoffensive way that allows you to fill a role in that group (e.g., you assume the role of the funny one, the sassy one, the leader, the rebel).

Cognitive Dissonance

We all have a desire to avoid cognitive dissonance, which is the state of having two conflicting beliefs, attitudes, or thoughts. No one wants to believe their actions contradict their self-image, so when your actions are forced down paths that contradict your internal mental model, you subtly rebuild your internal model to explain these actions.

For example, when you decide to switch jobs, you contextualize yourself as not enjoying your current job because it would create cognitive dissonance for you to leave a job you enjoyed. This is what makes your last few weeks at a job uniquely miserable and explains why it is difficult to work in such situations (in school environments, this is known as "senioritis").

Cognitive dissonance can be uniquely self-destructive when someone has a temporary health-related vice (obesity, low exercise, smoking, etc.), which they then incorporate into their internal character as being part of who they are, making it almost impossible to recover.

In a similar vein, cognitive dissonance can be uniquely challenging when we contextualize failing as part of who we are. Sometimes we fail at something big or a few times in a row and we begin to internalize that we are just the type of person who fails when they try things of that category. This is incredibly damaging as now, trying and winning at something will create cognitive dissonance and you will subconsciously sabotage your ability to win.

Personal Ego

The drive to see oneself in a positive light shapes many people's self-images. Our brains will go to enormous lengths to create a narrative that allows our internal self-images to be the heroes of our own stories. This method of developing a self-image can be uniquely insidious when it inevitably causes us to demonize positive traits we don't see ourselves as having.

A young boy in school who doesn't have many friends may be driven by his ego to contextualize himself as a "lone wolf outsider" who doesn't need to hang out with "those normies." He will begin to conceptualize normative behavior as intrinsically negative. His conceptualization may last long into his adult life and cause him to have difficulty building rapport when interviewing for jobs, dating, or building a support network of friends when moving to a new area.

If a man who has struggled financially lets his ego conceptualize himself as a "salt of the earth" type, he will begin to dismiss all wealthy people as immoral (potentially preventing him from even attempting to better his own situation).

Reinforcement

When we act in a certain way, we reinforce that aspect of our self-image. In many ways this is the same force as cognitive dissonance, but it is worth talking about separately, as it can dramatically snowball into very deleterious self-images through a process called avoidance.

Suppose one day you decide to not go to a party because the last time you went to a party you had a bad time. Now, you have "I am not the type of person who wants to be around a lot of people" lightly written into your self-image. Should you repeatedly make the same decision to not go to group events, you will reinforce that aspect of your self-image, thereby decreasing your likelihood of wanting to go to group events in the future.

Eventually, you will begin to make up stories about why you don't want to go to group events to justify the initial emotional impulse you feel not to (e.g., "I am not good at social situations" or "something horrible happened to me at a party and I will have flashbacks if I ever go to one"). If this initially innocuous behavior is left unchecked for decades, it can snowball into an aspect of your self-image that could seriously affect your ability to function within society.

Instruction

While it requires an enormous amount of effort for us to design our own self-images, it requires virtually no effort to have someone else tell us who we are and how we should interact with the world.

Brands and people alike leverage our vulnerability on this front to drive us to spend money on their products or do things that serve their personal interests. Advertisements tell us what we should find to be fun, how we should want to see ourselves, and what we should want in life. Authority figures, friends, family, colleagues, and even strangers tell us who we should and should not be.

Ironically, most of the external instruction we internalize as being part of our characters is not forced upon us but rather sought out. It is human nature to compulsively seek out anything that allows us to neatly categorize ourselves. This can be seen in everything from horoscopes to the Myers Briggs personality test, blood type personality tests (common in Asia), Tumblr tables that label your micro-sexuality, and online quizzes that tell us which TV show character we are.

It is difficult to emphasize just how strong the desire to label oneself is. Even if we manage to resist strict classification systems, every human feels the subtle pull of wanting to identify with the fictional characters we see as having some similarity to us (e.g., "I'm the 'Samantha' of my friend group"[7]), which can ultimately cause us to adopt other aspects of their archetype into our self-image.

What Forces Built Your Present Self-Image?

Take some time to consider how you came to view yourself as you see yourself today. Was it your ego? Your friends? Society?

Hopefully it is clear when you reflect on how you developed your current self-image that there is nothing uniquely "you" about that self-image. A "you" that you build for yourself is going to be a truer you than a self that has been pasted together

[7] As in: Samantha, from Sex in the City. We admit this dates us.

through serendipity. More importantly, a "you" that you consciously create will always be better at achieving your objective function.

How We Process Emotions

As we dive into the concept of a self-image and explore the role that self-image plays in what emotions we feel, it is worth understanding the specific pathway through which our self-image affects our emotional states. Here we will go into more detail about how emotions work and the limits of our abilities to influence them.

Note: When we talk about "emotions" in this section, we mean the term in the broadest possible sense: anything that could be referred to as a "feeling," or what a philosopher may call qualia.

Emotions appear to be broadly divisible into two categories:

- **Lower order emotions**: These are emotions that do not depend on our self-images and are either survival related, breeding related, or related to simple reward pathways in our brains. These include things like thirst, hunger, the desire to defecate, pain, lust, the fight or flight response, and addictions. The types of emotions that a fish may feel.

- **Higher order emotions**: These are the emotions that allow us to live as social animals. These include things like happiness, sadness, envy, anger, pride, jealousy, anxiousness, etc.

Lower order emotions are largely out of our control. They can only be inhibited or endured. When a yogi or someone says they have conquered hunger, what they mean is they have learned to endure and normalize the sensation of constant hunger to a point at which it no longer negatively affects them. This is not the case with higher order emotions, while these can be inhibited or endured, they can also be avoided or otherwise controlled entirely (unless they are the result of a systematic abnormal brain state like PTSD or depression).

It can sometimes be confusing as to whether an emotion is a higher order or lower order emotion because higher order emotions will often hijack lower order emotional pathways "to get the point across." For example, a person may be so sad their body begins to experience the lower order emotional pathway associated with nausea. Alternatively, a person may be so anxious that they begin to activate their lower order fight or flight response.

This hijacking of lower order emotional pathways can actually be incredibly damaging to our bodies, as they often were not evolved/designed to be activated for extended periods of time (for example: the fight or flight response activates our sympathetic nervous system, which is only designed to be activated for short periods of time, but because this response can be hijacked by anxiety, it can be left "left turned on" and shorten your lifespan by decades if left unaddressed). In these cases, the lower order emotion can be avoided by learning to control a higher order emotional pathway.

It is useful to remember that while both categories of emotions can be inhibited—pushed down so we don't have to experience them—suppressing emotions is cognitively taxing and will prevent you from inhibiting other impulses. It is also difficult to inhibit emotions if you are already inhabiting something else, like a desire to smoke or eat. Overriding emotions is also a temporary solution as our neural inhibition pathways will inevitably become exhausted. Thus, learning to manipulate our impulses and recurring emotional states is always better than just attempting to suppress them.

As discussed earlier, when you experience something that would lead to a higher order emotion, your unconscious mind checks it against your mental model of yourself in order to determine how you should feel about it. However, before your unconscious mind does that, it builds a story about the incoming information. It is this story that is being directly checked against our mental model, as our mental model cannot directly interact with sensory information. In other words, your mental model cannot interact with a picture you are looking at. It can only interact with the story you create about that picture.

Because it is the story we create about what we experience—and not the experiences themselves—that we check against our mental model to determine our emotional reaction, we can control our emotional reaction by changing the story we are telling ourselves about what we are experiencing. There are several ways we can contextualize any experience into stories that will affect us quite differently. This contextualization is entirely within our conscious control.

Recontextualization is something humans naturally do when dealing with tragedy. For example, when someone's parent dies, they may mitigate the grief they feel by creating a story about how it was really for the best ("Thank goodness she is no longer in pain"). Or when someone experiences a natural disaster, they contextualize it as part of God's plan, and because God's plan is ultimately a good thing, the negative emotions associated with experiencing the tragedy are mitigated.

Recontextualization is particularly useful for dealing with experiences that lead to an inconveniently high level of negative emotion. A good catch-all recontextualization one can use is: "This experience was actually positive, because it made me stronger."

Another method that can be used for handling powerful, otherwise-unavoidable negative emotions is mindfulness combined with patience. Simply remembering that strong emotions are rarely felt for more than a few minutes at a time can make them easier to endure. (This may not align with your memories of strong emotional states but if you take a moment to time one you will see it is true.)

Finally, despite all the stories we tell ourselves about how "we just want to be happy," it is important to remember just how much we instinctively desire to indulge in negative emotions when we feel it is appropriate to do so. Next time you are particularly angry about something, focus on just how easy it would be for you to let go of whatever it is you are angry about. It is your choice to stay angry.

When you let yourself get angry (or sad, jealous, vindictive, etc.), you are indulging in that emotion because you feel you have a good excuse to do so. A great example of this is when you share a moderately annoying experience with a friend, they say that you are justified in being angry. This almost always leads to an escalation from mild annoyance to full blown anger on your part, now that you feel you have been given permission to indulge.

There is a trend in pop/pseudo-psychology to claim benefits from indulging in emotional states that have been traditionally agreed to be negative, such as anger, jealousy, and sadness (largely due to the popularity of the children's movie "Inside Out," not due to actual research). We need to stress this is not the point we are making. It is generally bad to indulge in negative emotional states. Just because we are naturally compelled to indulge in negative emotions does not mean we are ever justified in doing so or that there is any evidence to suggest that doing so is beneficial. However, we are also not saying there isn't sometimes utility in allowing yourself to feel a negative emotion if it moves you closer to a goal (e.g., using anger to motivate yourself or using your sadness to socially persuade someone).

Traditionally negative emotional states *can* admittedly offer some short-term benefits when experienced in their moderate forms (moderate anxiety can produce heightened focus and attention, while moderate anger can create stimulus-induced analgesia, increasing your physical strength and inhibiting the parts of your brain involved in empathy, which makes you more rational). Nevertheless, there is no large or well-analyzed body of evidence suggesting that frequently indulging in negative emotions is in any way an objectively healthy way to live.

There is, however, a very large body of evidence that links frequently indulging in negative emotions to very serious health problems. Sustained anxiety or anger can lead to coronary disease and heart attacks, along with a number of other health issues. In contrast, there are no known health issues to sustained or extreme positive emotional states. In fact, the famous "nun study," which followed the diaries of 180 nuns, showed that happier nuns lived about ten years longer.

As entertaining and empowering as it may feel, pop psychology is not science and should not be regarded as such. For example, another common meme in pop psychology is the idea that punching things or breaking things will allow you to "let off anger" and help you deal with tense situations—yet repeated studies show that any sort of rumination, be it punching or venting, will only make the associated negative emotion worse.

Overlay States

In addition to higher and lower order emotions, we also experience an independent overlay state. These overlay states are not always given clear names, as they are not as distinct as emotions. Some words used to describe them include: malaise, being "in the zone," being "in a funk," being manic, or feeling foggy. Unlike higher and lower order emotions, your overlay state can last for hours or even days. Moreover, these states heavily affect your cognitive capacity (e.g., your ability to "think clearly") as well as modulate the threshold of stimulation required to feel a higher order emotion. For example, when you are in a state of malaise, the threshold to feel sadness is lower and you will feel sad about things that otherwise wouldn't bother you.

Overlay states are caused by "system wide" effects on the brain that can be influenced by factors ranging from diet to the time of day, hormones, physical fitness level, and whether you have the flu.

Positive overlay states can be created through simple "life hygiene." This includes eating healthy food, exercising, meditating, maintaining good sleep hygiene, giving to charity (yes, there is research showing this raises baseline happiness), having meaningful work, maintaining regular social interaction with people you like, having a sense of purpose, knowing what you want from life, etc. If you are attempting to maximize a certain overlay state, the best method is to record daily activities and record your daily overlay state. You can use this information to look for positive trends between the two. One surprising thing that results from overlay state monitoring is the realization that actions which do not feel good in the moment, such as caloric restriction, exercise, charitable giving, hard work, or social interaction, can ultimately have a very positive effect on your overlay state.

As mentioned above, having a sense of purpose will also help to affect your overlay state. The objective function, ideologies, and persona you cultivate as a result of applied pragmatic thought may come in very handy for creating a better overlay state, as studies indicate one of the best ways to maximize your overlay state is to feel there is purpose to your life. (Note: The scientific community does not use the term overlay state.)

Note: A persistent negative overlay state in the face of normal "life hygiene" can be created by certain mental illnesses and will require psychopharmacology and professional behavioral therapy to remedy. Not seeking help when you notice yourself in such a condition is akin to not going to a doctor when you realize you have advanced pneumonia. Sure, you may be able to "tough it out," but you may also end up dead.

The Effects of Overlay States on Emotions

Overlay states are often talked about in terms of emotions, but while overlay states can affect emotional states, they are not exactly emotional states themselves. A person can have so much of a higher order emotion that that emotion hijacks a lower order emotional pathway (e.g., a person can be so sad they feel physical pain), but a person cannot have so much of an overlay state that they feel an emotion (a person cannot be at such a high level of malaise that they feel sadness).

Instead, overlay states affect the threshold of stimulation required to experience certain emotional states. A person in a strong overlay state will need much less stimulus to feel happy, sad, angry, or any other higher (or lower) order emotion.

In sum, you experience a higher order emotional state through the following pathway:
To experience a higher order emotion:

1. You experience something
2. You tell yourself a story about what you experienced
3. You reference that story against your mental model to determine a level of emotional output
4. If that emotional output level is higher than the threshold created by your overlay state, you will experience said emotion

For example:

1. You notice you are the only person sitting alone in the movie theater
2. You tell yourself a story about how this means you are more alone than most other people
3. You see yourself as the type of person who doesn't want to be alone, so you release a small level of sadness output
4. Typically, this level of sadness output would not be experienced as sadness but because

your overlay state is "hormonal" due to being pregnant your threshold for experiencing sadness is unusually low and you begin crying

When you regard overlay states as filters changing the threshold needed to experience an emotion, it makes sense people are likely born with quite divergent "default" overlay states. Specifically, some studies have backed the idea of happiness set point theory, which essentially claims people are born with different thresholds of stimulus required to experience happiness. The most famous studies associated with this theory follow people after major life events—such as winning the lottery or marriage—and demonstrate that after a short period of time, people return to the same level of happiness they experienced before the event. In essence, this theory finds people gravitate toward a level of happiness that they developed very early in life, either through genetics, through in utero conditions, or throughout early life experiences.

The only thing that can affect the level of positive emotion you experience in your life as much as your self-image is your "default" overlay state. Fortunately, studies have shown this state can be nudged both up and down in terms of this threshold sensitivity. Events such as the loss of a child/spouse, or continued unemployment, will nudge your threshold for happiness up (making it permanently harder to experience happiness), while actions such as prolonged charitable activities and exercise will nudge your happiness threshold down (making it permanently easier to experience happiness).

Directly Stimulating Positive Emotional States

Let's explore how we can maximize our positive emotional experiences while keeping this model in mind.

(1) You experience something
(2) You tell yourself a story about what you experienced
(3) You reference that story against your mental model to determine a level of emotional output
(4) If that emotional output level is higher than the threshold created by your overlay state, you will experience said emotion

This section will be divided into two parts: maximizing pursuits that make us feel good—things we do in the physical world—and maximizing experiences that make us feel good—the way we relate to experiences we are not currently living through either as aspects of our memory or imagination.

Maximizing Pursuits that Make You Feel Good

Maximizing stage (1) "you experience something," seems deceptively simple. Just put yourself in a position to experience things that make you feel positive emotions, right? In practice, maximizing step (1) is more difficult to do than one may think. This difficulty ultimately demonstrates just how much work the "maximizing positive emotional states" objective function really is.

Despite what we tell ourselves about wanting to be happy, we are horrendous at actively pursuing experiences that make us genuinely happy. This is due both to the fact that we often just refuse to take the initiative to seek happy experiences and because humans are not good at identifying what kinds of activities will make them happy.

Take stock of the things you have done this week to make yourself happy. Now reflect on how much happiness you felt during each of those experiences. How much were you smiling uncontrollably? How much were you laughing? How much love did you feel? Now take stock of the last thing you spent over $5,000 on to make yourself happy (a trip for example) and ask yourself the same questions. How much were you smiling uncontrollably? How much were you laughing?

How much love did you feel? If you are like most people, if you are like us, your answer will be: "very little."

Why do we spend money and time doing things we tell ourselves we are doing to make ourselves happy but don't actually bring us much happiness? Because we spend very little time consciously observing how happy specific types of experiences make us on average. Instead, we make five common mistakes when categorizing activities and expenditures that bring us happiness.

Mistake 1:
Instead of focusing on how happy an activity makes us on average, we focus more on specific memories in which we had a uniquely high level of positive emotion. We then categorize whatever activity we were undertaking when we reached that uniquely high state of positive emotion as an activity that is likely to on average give us a high positive emotional state. For example, we may categorize going out to a nightclub as a happiness-generating experience because we have a couple very positive memories associated with nightclubs—even if most of the time when we go to nightclubs, we do very little other than go through the motions of what we *feel* like we are supposed to do in that environment.

Mistake 2:

We also have a problem with lying to ourselves about how happy certain things and activities make us. If we spend a lot of money or effort on an experience, we are unlikely to admit to ourselves that the experience was mostly unpleasant. We will find it very hard to acknowledge that we could have experienced more positive moments doing something that costs less time and money. For example, if we spend a significant amount of money on an expensive trip, we are unlikely to admit to ourselves that we would have been happier staying home and binge reading good books (or doing something else familiar and comforting). As a result, we often end up chasing experiences that are expensive or inconvenient simply because they are expensive and inconvenient.

Mistake 3:
Sometimes people will tell themselves they enjoy an experience because that experience is tied to something they are addicted to and their subconscious is looking for an excuse to indulge in the addiction. For example, someone addicted to gambling may categorize sitting in front of a slot machine and pulling a lever as a positive emotional experience even when in reality they get almost no positive emotional stimulation from the experience, while someone addicted to alcohol may categorize events that allow them to become intoxicated in a socially acceptable setting as enjoyable, even if

they would gain more enjoyment by staying home and getting drunk while reading a good book.

When looking for experiences we have convinced ourselves we enjoy because they are associated with something addictive, remember that most human addictions are not substance-based but a result of intermittent reward pathways.

The classic study demonstrating how powerfully addictive intermediate reward pathways are was conducted by B. F. Skinner and showed that if you give a rat a lever that releases a food pellet (reward) whenever it is pressed, the rat will press it when it wants food. If, however, the lever releases food only *sometimes*, the rat will get a large dopamine rush in addition to (occasional) food and will become addicted to pushing the lever, sometimes doing nothing but pushing the lever all day long. The dopamine rush caused by intermittent rewards is like any other drug, forming dependency in the user and eventually no longer yielding the positive emotion which led to the addiction in the first place. In their most raw form in humans, interment reward pathways are what cause gambling addictions and make it difficult for people to leave abusive relationships in which the partner is sometimes nice.

However, there are many less obviously destructive activities we become addicted to through intermittent reward pathways—things we tell ourselves we do for fun when the activity actually brings us very little happiness. A classic example is a simple mobile phone or social media game (Farmville being the archetype here). However, intermittent reward pathways are also core to many activities that give us other types of enjoyment, such as golf, posting to social media, playing video games, watching sports, etc. Note that these activities don't have features to recommend them on their own; an intermittent reward addiction accounts for at least part of their enjoyment and popularity.

Mistake 4:
When you are on autopilot, you will naturally gravitate towards activities that reinforce your self-image. While sometimes fun, these activities are rarely the most enjoyable options available. For example, a person who sees themselves as an intellectual bohemian may go to a museum not because they enjoy the content of the museum, but because they enjoy doing an activity that reinforces the way they see themselves. Whenever we do an activity that reinforces our self-images, we experience a moderate amount of activation in the reward pathways of our brains and feel good. This is a normal part of processing higher order emotions.

However, social media has caused a disruption in this behavior pattern and can lead us to expend inordinately large amounts of time, effort, and resources on activities that don't lead to sustainable positive emotional states. While reinforcing your own self-image provides you with a moderate activation of your brain's reward pathways, having someone else validate your self-image provides you with a much larger hit to those reward pathways. Thus, while going to a museum may activate a bit of a self-identified intellectual's reward pathway, posting a picture at a museum and having someone else comment how intellectual that person is provides them with a much greater reward. The problem created by this social media validation is compounded when you consider that it is an intermediate reward (we don't *always* get rewarding feedback when we post something online) that fits all the criteria for a highly addictive reward pathway. Essentially, people become addicted to having others validate their self-images through social media without recognizing it as an addiction.

Outside of the imminent danger of becoming addicted to others' validation of your self-image on social media, there is a less insidious risk that the type of content you post to social media will alter your memory of an event and cause you to believe you were happy doing something that actually was not much fun at all.

Just yesterday, we walked by a large, expensive-looking party and noticed that not a single guest was smiling except when taking selfies. Today, when they post those selfies online and tell all their friends how much fun they had at this expensive party, they will begin to build a false memory of their experience at the event. This false memory will be reinforced every time they go through their old photos and see images of themselves smiling alongside comments and tags indicating how much fun they were having.

Essentially, when a person posts to social media about an event (whether it be a trip, a nightclub, or a fancy party) they almost never comment on how mediocre the experience is. Instead, people mostly post and share photos in which they are smiling and having a great time; after all, everyone needs to know how great their lives are! This would not be a significant problem if this behavior pattern were applied equally to all the things we did to make ourselves happy, but it is rare for us to post things which make us happy that won't also make others jealous or think our lives are great.

It is rare for someone to post a picture of themselves content at home alone with a beer curled up on the sofa with their cat while watching cartoons. The reality is that most people would be much happier doing something at home alone than hobnobbing at a fancy party, however due to the role social media plays in their lives, they are more likely to remember the fancy party as a happy moment.

Mistake 5:

Finally, it is very common for us to categorize an experience as something that makes us happy because it made us happy in the past—even if we are no longer capable of deriving happiness from the experience. As we age, the things that make us happy change. The most significant example of this phenomenon is the decline in "play behavior" many mammals (including humans) experience over time.

All young mammals exhibit something called play behavior. If you have ever owned a puppy, you will immediately recognize this behavior and will also be aware that, as the dog aged, its proclivity towards play behavior declined. The repertoire of activities that made the dog happy changed as it aged and the instinctual drive towards play behavior declined. Humans also experience a decline in a drive towards play behavior with age.

Our gradually disappearing play behavior manifests itself as a shift in our default overlay state that, as we age, raises the threshold of happiness associated with frenetic physical activity, curiosity, and imagination, and lowers the threshold of happiness that comes from serenity, relaxation, and nurturing others. Despite this shift that makes physical/curious/imaginary play less enjoyable over time, some people still gravitate toward youth-optimized forms of play out of habit.

All five of these potential pitfalls can be easily avoided by regularly trying new activities and critically thinking about how happy an activity makes you feel in the moment. Be open to the fact that what brings you a positive emotional experience today may be something that you detested in the past. Just because you *remember* having a great experience doing something in the past doesn't mean you will genuinely enjoy that same experience today. Even if something seems like the type of thing you would like, it is still worth paying attention to whether or not you actually enjoy it.

Maximizing Experiences that Make you Feel Good

Maximizing experiences that make you feel good does not just involve careful selection of those experiences most likely to make you feel good. It is important to remember that step (1) on the pathway that leads to an emotional output is not: "you participate in an activity," but rather "you experience something." This experience does not have to be something you are actually doing in the moment but can be completely in your imagination.

Even though imagined scenarios are completely within our control, they ultimately—almost comically—generate more negative emotions in the average person than positive emotions. This not only comes through ruminating on how a potential action could end up embarrassing you, how a past action lost you an opportunity, or how terrible a potential future could be but also comes from remembering positive experiences.

Often when people attempt to ruminate on the happy moments of their lives, they nail step (1), the experience, successfully remembering a happy moment from the past, but then at step (2), the interpretation of that experience, they tell themselves a story about how sad it is they aren't experiencing those happy things right now, which evokes a negative emotion.

This is ironic, as most people don't ruminate on sad events in their past and tell themselves stories about how happy they are they are not experiencing them in the present. Both steps (1), what you are remembering, and step (2), the story you tell yourself about that memory, are entirely within your control. At any point, you can choose to remember the happiest moments of your life and be happy you had those experiences—or remember the worst moments of your life and choose to feel relieved you aren't experiencing them right now.

But our experiences are not limited to things we experienced in the past, things we might experience, and things we are experiencing right now. We are also capable of experiencing things that are 100% imaginary. This is instinctively obvious to us as children. Children can easily reason that it would be more fun to experience themselves fighting off the alien scourge overwhelming the citadel alongside a crack troop of space marines than to experience the mundane act of playing on a boring playground with their friends.

One of the greatest things about being human is you can mentally experience almost anything you want at any time. Right now, you could close your eyes and imagine yourself sitting on a beach, listening to the waves, feeling the wind in your hair, and sipping on a frozen margarita. You probably just don't have a habit of imagining things anymore.

With age, many people stop expending the mental effort required to create their own imaginary experiences. Older people instead rely on the crutch of books and television to escape reality. Part of this is due to the subconscious realization that sometimes people who professionally imagine things are just better at it, and that we gain more value from indulging in someone else's imagined world if we can share that world with others in our social circle. Still, we encourage you to remember that you have the power experience any world you choose to live in, at least for a while.

Recontextualizing Your Experiences to Maximize Positive Emotions

Just as what you are experiencing—step (1)—is *often* within your conscious control, how you contextualize those experiences, step (2) is *always* within your conscious control. The story we tell ourselves about what we are experiencing is what our internal model references when determining how we should feel. If we go back to the woman in sitting alone in the movie theater, we can see that there are many stories she could tell herself about that experience other than: "Everyone else here has friends; I am so alone," such as, "I am so glad I don't have to share my popcorn!" or "Thank goodness I won't have someone whispering commentary to me through the movie!"

The ever-popular cinematic family, the Addams Family, present a great demonstration of how powerful recontextualization can be and how jarringly rare it is. The strangest thing about the Addams Family is not the occasionally supernatural events that happen in their lives, but the fact they choose to contextualize things differently than most people and they have different mental models against which they test that contextualization. For example, if Morticia sees a wilted flower, she decides to contextualize that experience as a positive one. Subconsciously, we all realize that choice is not a supernatural one, but a choice any of us could make at any time.

It is almost comically easy to experience happiness whenever you want, even though only one third of Americans describe themselves as happy. You could choose to be experiencing literally the happiest place and thing you can imagine right now, but instead you have chosen not to. Realizing this shakes many people from an objective function based around maximizing positive emotions because what they really meant when asserting that positive emotions have inherent value was, "I want to choose whatever objective function means I don't have to change anything about how I live my life."

Realizing that positive emotional states are always within their grasp assuming they are willing to put in a large amount of effort (and don't have a systematic brain abnormality) makes people rethink the judgment call that they have an imperative to maximize positive emotional states in themselves. This brings us back to the core point of this chapter: even though it is possible to maintain a near constant happy state through sustained mental effort, it is always going to be easier to create a sustained happy state by simply altering the self-image against which an experience and interpretation is tested. For this reason, most of your time when reading this section should be focused on deciding what self-image you want and how you will create that self-image.

The following section portion is skippable, as it isn't actually useful in choosing who you want to be or controlling your emotional state and is entirely conjecture based on one of the author's experiences building neural networks. However, if you do like this section, you are likely to really like The Pragmatist's Guide to Sexuality, where we have many similar discussions.

The glaring question raised by the above four-step system for emotional reactions is: Why, when we remember happy memories, does our brain default to creating negative stories about how sad it is we aren't experiencing those things right now? In other words, what creates the default pathways our brain takes when we are not actively attempting to influence how we think about something?

Looking at this from the perspective of a neural network, we can begin to get an idea of what may be happening. Neural networks attempt to recreate brain pathways in computers to understand why they behave as they do. Simple neural networks are often based around an input, an output, and a system in between the two that learns how to maximize a certain output based on various inputs. This system is neither conscious, nor designed to prioritize one flavor of output over another (e.g., happy vs. sad) it is only supposed to maximize a given output (e.g., emotion).

If we define the various states this closed system can take as autopilot choices for how we are contextualizing an experience and ask ourselves: "What output is this closed emotion generation system optimizing for?" the answer becomes clear. When it is not being disrupted by the conscious parts of your mind, this system is optimized to enter whatever state will lead to the maximum possible emotional output. For example, if you think of a happy memory, the emotional signal created by deciding to be sad about that experience being over is stronger than the emotional signal created by a decision to be happy that the experience happened at all. The system, which has no reason to favor "happy" over "sad," will merely enter whatever state causes the strongest signal.

However, a practicing neuroscientist editor argued for a different explanation centered around negativity bias: "That negative emotions are overall generally perceived as stronger than positive emotions. Your most negative emotion possible is really much more salient than your most positive emotion possible. So, when presented with a memory that brings happiness about having experienced it and sadness that it isn't being experienced in the moment at about equal levels, the negative emotion will be perceived as stronger." Obviously, we disagree, finding the concept of "positive" and "negative" emotions to be somewhat arbitrary and subject to change, but it is worth at least providing readers with a couple of possible explanations for this curious tendency in humans.

Optimizing for Remembered Experiences

Just as a better understanding of how humans process emotions can help people achieve some objective functions, a better understanding of how humans create "remembered experiences" is useful in achieving others.

What do we mean by "remembered experiences"? Consider an experience in which you are blackout drunk, but still able to process emotions and the world around you. That experience is not recorded and completely wiped from your memory. Does that forgotten experience still "count" towards your objective function? Alternatively, what about something you experience in a dream that is quickly wiped from your memory? What about something you experienced but have very little memory of weeks after?

A good way to test whether your objective function assigns more value to remembered experiences is to ask yourself: If there were two people who each lived for 100 years and had equally happy lives, but one slept twenty hours a day and the other only slept eight hours a day, which life would you prefer to have lived? As most do not count sleeping as "experiencing life," they would choose the life of the person who slept only eight hours a night and had more total hours of conscious experiences they could remember.

Sleeping and being blackout drunk aren't the only times our ability to remember the world is turned off. Almost anyone who drives is familiar with the phenomenon of highway hypnosis, in which you get in a car and find yourself arriving at your destination without much memory of driving there (it is particularly noticeable when you end up at an old workplace/home and don't realize you had been going the wrong way until you arrive). A person in this state is not experiencing the world consciously in part because they are doing something they have done a hundred times before and their brain has turned off its "recording processes." Highway hypnosis aside, how many unique commutes to/from home and work or school can you remember?

Highway hypnosis is clearly an extreme case. However, there are many times we experience something and then forget it just days or weeks later. If you weight such experiences less than others, there are fortunately heuristics you can use to create experiences you will remember.

The simplest of these heuristics is to pursue as many novel experiences as possible. People remember much more about events in which we are exposed to novel stimuli. This is apparent with a little bit of retrospection: Can you remember exactly what you were doing five weeks ago today? Alternately, can you remember exactly what you did on day two of the last trip you took? Chances are you remember much more about the trip you took than a random sampling from your everyday life.

A similar phenomenon happens on a grander scale through something called a "reminiscence bump." Originally, it was assumed this was a strange phenomenon whereby elderly people remembered their teens through their thirties better than any other part of their lives in old age. Later studies showed that if you moved the most defining and novel events of a person's life to a different time (people who migrated to a different country in their 30s for example), the reminiscence bump would move as well.

Some argue that this enhanced ability to remember certain times in our lives is due to the number of novel things we experienced during those times, while others argue that reminiscence bumps are a product of the formative role those experiences played in creating our personal identities.

Each explanation likely carries an element of truth. We can remember life more clearly when experiencing novel stimuli and when rewriting our identities. One of the most famous (though now slightly more dubious) theories in psychology is that we form uniquely vivid memories called flashbulb memories when we are presented with an event or information that is unique, emotionally arousing, and character building (news of 9/11 for instance).

Should you want to maximize the extent to which you "experience" life, you should therefore opt for novel and formative experiences whenever possible. When deciding between two date activities with your spouse—such as staying in and watching a movie, something you have done every date night for the past year but love doing, or going on a guided tour through a local factory, something you have some interest in but probably won't enjoy as much—remember that perhaps you should not only be weighing how much positive emotion will be generated by an experience, but also how many novel memories that experience will create.

Why do our brains erase non-novel memories? Your brain tries to save as much room as possible and will not record every time you do something as a new and separate experience but instead will group similar experiences together as a single "memory," such as every time you drive to a friend's house. If you decide to mix things up a bit and do the same experience in a slightly different way, you will trigger a phenomenon called "retrieval induced forgetting," in which your brain erases some of the memory of the original route you took to your friend's house and writes over it with the memory of the new route.

All of this may be fantastic from an efficiency standpoint, but it means that all those habitual things you do for fun will be constantly overwritten. For example, if you do a date night every night with your spouse in which you watch a different movie you will remember these experiences less than if you did something totally different every night.

(Whenever we mention a mainstream psychological phenomenon by name there are going to be disagreements in the psychological community as to how the phenomenon works and this is one of those instances. It is not worth our time to go into detail on these, as for our purposes the only thing that matters it that retrieval induced forgetting exists.)

Thus, if an important aspect of your objective function is maximizing the amount of "memory" generated, you would benefit from constantly moving to new cities, creating new homes, and reinventing who you are.

Finally, the vividness and detail with which you remember something is not tied to the accuracy of what you are remembering (despite common intuition to the contrary). Several studies have shown that while people have uniquely vivid memories of where they were on 9-11, those memories aren't necessarily accurate. Essentially, every time you reflect on a memory, you are re-recording your reflection—creating a copy of a copy—and the accuracy of these copies will degrade over time. Furthermore, because you reflect on emotionally charged memories more often, they are more likely to be inaccurate but very vivid.

Keep in mind when deciding how to maximize your memories whether you are maximizing for just the number and vividness of memories, in which case emotionally charged experiences are superior, or whether you are maximizing for accurate memories, in which case novel, life-changing experiences are superior.

How Self-Images Affect Our Perception

Let us return to self-images, how they can be built, and how they affect us.

In addition to influencing the way we process emotions and act when we are on autopilot, our self-images can filter the information we are capable of accepting and internalizing. In contrast to our ideologies, which act as filters on what we are willing to accept as true, our self-images act as filters on our perceptions of the world, blocking information before it ever accesses our mental landscape.

For example, someone who maintains the idea that they are "a good person" at the core of their self-image will have a very difficult time critically thinking about their actions and whether or not they are indeed "good." A self-identified "good person" may be able to run the words: "maybe I am not actually a good person" through their mental-scape's phonological loop (the part of our working memory that plays words as we think them) while reading this page, but they will not be able to seriously entertain the concept that their actions may not be "good." This person runs the risk of ultimately defining "good" as "the things they do," which can justify horrific actions.

The perception filter your personal identity creates isn't necessarily a bad thing. It depends on your ideology. For example, someone who sees themselves as scientifically minded may dismiss all talk of auras out of hand without wasting processing power on the concept. Someone who sees themselves as politically correct may dismiss any scientific evidence that would lead to racist or sexist conclusions. Depending on your ideology, such out-of-hand dismissal of stimuli may or may not be a bad thing. Most people would not want to dismiss something out of hand just because it conflicted with their self-image; however, it is conceivable that such a person exists, and we are attempting to remain unbiased.

This perception filter created by our core identities is not absolute. Sometimes information that clashes with our core identities is so voluminous or compelling it breaks through and we must contend with it. When this happens, our natural response is to become angry or agitated and attribute negative associations with the source of this information. For example, when someone who identifies as intelligent is categorically proven wrong, they will become very angry, accuse the person who proved them wrong of cheating, or attack the source of the information's credibility rather than internalize that they may not actually be as intelligent as they would like to believe.

Self-Image Creation and Hygiene

When building an ideal self-image for yourself, it is important to revisit how our self-images affect us. Our self-images (i.e., our internal mental models of ourselves) have six primary effects:

- During social interaction, we subconsciously reference our self-images to determine how we feel about what is happening and what our "default" responses will be.
- When making major and minor life decisions, our initial emotional impulse will be to do whatever is in line with our self-images (these decisions can be as big as determining how you respond to a marriage proposal or as small as determining what to post to Facebook).
- We seek out activities (and information) that reinforce our self-images. Taking part in activities that reinforce your self-image creates positive emotional feedback.
- Our self-images influence the emotions we feel. We react emotionally to situations in the way we would expect someone with a self-image like ours to react.
- When we are presented with information, we can easily ignore and avoid processing information that does not conform to our self-images. This information will never be delivered to our conscious minds. For example, someone who sees being a communist as core to their identity may travel through a communist country and genuinely not mentally register evidence suggesting that people are suffering.
- When we are presented with difficult-to-ignore information that conflicts with our self-images, we will become viscerally angry and apply a negative association to the source of said information. Rather than process this information

properly, we will immediately begin generating reasons why it must be wrong and ruminating on how much we hate the source of the information.

The first step in altering some aspect of our self-images involves acknowledging that the thing we have decided to alter is part of our self-images. There is no clear map of our self-images we can reference. Instead, we must build an understanding of our self-images by working backwards, using the above six points for reference.

For example, if you read an article that portrays a certain political party in a negative light and you find yourself getting angry and thinking about what a partisan hack the author must be, you have almost certainly internalized your political affiliation into your self-image. If, when scrolling through your online post history, you notice a lot of "intellectual" posts (and you had not consciously been trying to look intellectual), then being intellectual is probably part of your self-image.

As you begin to piece together characteristics of the internal model you have of yourself, you can begin to identify the pieces of it that are detrimental to your objective function. These aspects of your identity will typically cause one of three things:

- Unnecessary negative emotions
- Unproductive impulses
- An inability to process information required to help you achieve your objective function

The first two points are easy to recognize, if difficult to change. During the course of a day, if you find yourself reacting emotionally in an unproductive way, or say something in a social situation you recognize as detrimental, determine what aspect of your self-image lead you to react that way and then note it as something you want to change.

The third point is the hardest to identify as something you want to change, as it almost always represents something you like about yourself. You may become angry because you read something that ran contrary to a political belief you had internalized into your self-image, but you probably internalized that belief into your self-image because of a strong affinity for it. Unfortunately, it will be almost impossible to effectively spread the belief because if it is part of your identity, you will never be able to empathize with the thought process of someone who doesn't hold it. If you can't empathize with the thought process of someone who holds different beliefs, you cannot convince them they are wrong.

When identifying what you want to change about yourself, remember that just because something makes you sad, scared, or anxious does not mean a related element of your self-identity needs to be eliminated or changed. Sometimes negative emotional reactions benefit you. There is only one emotional state that is a universally negative:

offense. Taking genuine personal offense to something yields zero utility towards any objective function and primarily serves to prevent people from attempting to understand viewpoints that differ from their own, (although one may certainly occasionally fake offense to one's advantage).

You should be able to adjust your internal self-image on your own, with a spouse, or with a friend. However, if it is easier for you to work with someone who knows this model well or who you do not know, you can always reach out to us directly through admin@pragmatist.guide we are always happy to chat with readers in exchange for honest reviews on Amazon (haha).

Unproductive Self-images

As you validate your current self-image, keep an eye out for counterproductive elements that may have wormed their way into your self-image, several of which are summarized below. These summaries should help you quickly spot potential areas for improvement in yourself, as nearly everyone has at least one of these elements in their organically formed self-images.

As you read, recall that an attack on a self-image is not an attack on you, but will almost always feel like one. Our first impulse when hearing/reading that our self-image may be wrong is to lash out against the source of that information. We encourage you to watch for this reaction in yourself as you read through this list.

Failure or Helplessness as Part of Who You Are

It is possible for someone to build failure or helplessness into the core of their mental model. This phenomenon is called learned helplessness and has been observed in a few mammal species in addition to humans. For example, if rats/dogs are exposed to electrical shocks they cannot escape, they will not attempt to escape them when later given the opportunity. In humans, learned helplessness occurs when an individual experiences failure at a specific task enough times to internalize the inevitability of failing at that task as part of who they are. Unless they challenge this aspect of their identity, succeeding at said task becomes next to impossible.

Have you ever said: "I am just bad at X, so there is no point in trying anymore"? This can be in relation to anything from learning another language to overcoming obesity. If this is an explanation you have presented in the past, it is likely that you have incorporated inevitable failure at certain tasks into your self-identity.

Note: Learning to succeed at a task at which you have repeatedly failed involves more than altering your self-image to that of someone who can succeed at this task. You will also need to determine what other systematic factors contributed to your repeated failure and address them. For example, if you repeatedly end up in bad relationships, it is worth examining specifically what might have gone wrong with the common variable (you). Did you do a poor job at sourcing your partners? Did you vet them poorly? Did you act in a way that encouraged your partners to treat you poorly? Did you not leave them immediately when it became clear that the relationship had no future? (For a deep exploration of relationships, check out *The Pragmatist's Guide to Relationships*—a sequel to this guide.)

External Locus of Control

A person with an external locus of control does not assume personal responsibility for things that happen to them, assigning responsibility instead to other people and external circumstances (e.g., "the economy," "racism," or "millennials."). When asked why they are still single, someone with an external locus of control might say it's "because girls are all crazy." If asked why they can't get a job, they may reply "immigrants took all the jobs." Studies have repeatedly shown that individuals who adopt an external locus of control are less happy, less successful, less empathetic, and less likable.

External loci of control are uniquely difficult to shake, as in many cases, good and bad things that happen to us really *are* a product of external forces. Forces outside of our control may make life harder for us than other people but failing to meet this increased standard is still 100% our fault.

Perceptions of fairness often influence whether someone develops an internal or external locus of control. Those who strongly believe the world should be "fair" and believe that fairness has inherent value trend toward external loci of control. Those who do not view fairness as having any inherent value and who are comfortable with the idea that the world is not fair are more likely to develop an internal locus of control.

If you want to choose to believe that the world would be better if it were fair, then we encourage you to ensure you have a very good logical reason to hold that belief, because anyone living life with an expectation of fairness from the world will both be less happy and less successful in any conventional sense.

If you are systematically oppressed, it will be even more difficult for you to maintain an internal locus of control, as you must regularly confront the setbacks associated with an unfair world. That said, even if your objective function in life involves fighting systematic oppression, you will still be better off if you cultivate an internal locus of control, take personal responsibility for your life and circumstances, and accept that—even in a world with no systemic oppression—unfairness will be endemic. There is no conceivable situation in a modern Western society in which an external locus of control will help you achieve your objective function (unless your objective function revolves around being as helpless as possible which seems unlikely).

Though some develop an external locus of control in response to real, material oppression, most people with an external locus of control are not oppressed. Most people with an external locus of control merely refuse to take responsibility for their own failures. These are people who get dumped and blame it on the next person their old partner dates. These are investors who lose money and blame it on the market. These are entrepreneurs who fail to raise money and blame it on investors being too narrow-minded to realize their vision. A person with an external locus of control will always find a reason why their failures aren't their own.

A good way to determine whether you have an external locus of control is to list the last five major setbacks in your life and the reasons behind those setbacks. If two or more of these setbacks aren't your fault, you have an external locus of control. Getting rid of an external locus of control is extremely difficult. Conceptualizing yourself as a victim (either of fate or oppression) can be deeply alluring. Victimhood gives you power by allowing you to dismiss negative feedback out of hand, empowering you to accuse the source of bias or ignorance, and allowing you to blame your failings on anything but yourself. Victimhood allows you to feel like you are succeeding (in relative terms) regardless of your actual achievements.

Vice-Oriented Self-images

Beware of self-images that incorporate a vice as being "part of who you are" (smoking, drinking, obesity, violence, drugs, etc.). Incorporating a vice into your self-image makes it almost impossible to shake bad habits and can cause you to conceptualize negative influences in your life as positive influences. Worse still, vice-oriented self-images will make you conceptualize people trying to help you as people trying to attack the core of who you are and will create a perception filter that makes it difficult for you to recognize ways to better yourself.

Examples of vice-oriented self-images are people who see themselves as "a bad boy" and people who internalize being overweight as part of who they are as a person (e.g., "I'm fat and fabulous!"). It is not uncommon for formerly overweight people to relapse into old eating habits, arguing that they "did not feel like themselves" when they were skinny. In the same vein, someone may tie something like smoking or drinking to their sense of masculinity and feel less masculine upon quitting.

These kinds of self-images are uniquely seductive in that they turn a trait of yours that would lead you to feeling bad about yourself into points of pride. We would normally encourage such a recontextualization—one that allowed an individual to turn a source of negative feelings into one of positive feelings—if those negative feelings didn't exist for a reason: to help you not kill yourself.

I need X to feel X

All humans are driven to give in to our impulses. This is why these impulses exist, after all. We have an impulse to eat so we don't starve. We have an impulse to procrastinate so we save energy. We have an impulse to consume more of an addictive substance because it has hijacked reward pathways in our brains that are supposed to motivate us to be productive.

The more constant an impulse is, the more time we have to create arguments as to why we should give into it. Everyone rationalizes the occasional surrender a base impulse. This rationalization only becomes problematic when we incorporate it into our identities. Once someone does this, it becomes nearly impossible to permanently suppress said impulse.

Examples of people who incorporate these rationalizations include:

- People who come to see themselves as procrastinators
- People who argue they can only become creative/productive/happy after smoking pot/drinking alcohol/using some other controlled substance
- People who tell themselves they can only get work done if they take regular breaks (e.g., for social media, walks, whatever)

While these arguments are logically wrong, we are willing to accept them as they come packaged with strong impulse. If we surrender to these arguments enough times, we run the risk of accidentally internalizing these arguments into our mental model.

Fortunately, this is not a particularly difficult aspect of an internal model to change (assuming you are willing to challenge yourself). These illogical excuses can be easily spotted when you are actively looking for them. For example, when you are procrastinating, you know it; you have merely allowed yourself to lose the mental battle to overcome it.

A Self-Image of a Lower Status Than That You Occupy

It is common for someone to assign a certain social status or level of competency to their self-image. When someone's position in society does not align with the status of their self-image, they will feel as if they are an imposter and that eventually others will identify them as not belonging. This is often referred to as "imposter syndrome" and is frequent enough—especially amongst high performing groups—that Stanford Business School must hold workshops on it for all incoming students.

Despite common perceptions to the contrary, it is rarely counterproductive to see yourself as deserving a higher status or position than you presently hold—so long as you are willing to work to attain the competency this status/position commands. Ultimately, choosing to see yourself as having a higher status or position than you presently have may give you just the motivation and confidence you need to push yourself and overcome your weaknesses.

Believing you deserve a higher position than you presently hold is only damaging when you maintain an external locus of control (almost no combination of mental models is more likely to lead to failure than a belief that you deserve more from life and an unwillingness to assume personal responsibility for your shortcomings). However, if you are willing to accept responsibility for your shortcomings and failures, it is almost always worth learning to believe you deserve better.

The Self-Image of a Perfectionist / Someone Who Does Not Fail Often

The self-image of a perfectionist or "perfect student/athlete/worker/etc." is usually acquired after repeated successes early in life and is incredibly damaging. This may seem odd, as one would assume someone who does not see themselves as capable of failure would have more confidence and would strive to achieve greater things. This is not how this perception plays out in practice, unfortunately.

This self-image becomes damaging because the easiest way for such a person's subconscious to ensure their reality aligns with their self-image is to ensure they don't attempt things at which they may fail. People who see themselves as naturally perfect in some way will find themselves unable to take risks and ultimately languish in a life of mediocrity. For this reason, many parenting guides now advocate praising children for being hardworking and persistent rather than smart or talented.

If you ever find yourself not taking a risk due to the possibility of a failure scenario in which only your ego stands to get hurt, you are likely infected with some aspect of this self-image. This weakness can be overcome by actively putting yourself in situations in which you may fail so you become used to the feeling and understand that failure alone is not something to avoid.

The Self-Image of a Good Person

Establishing the belief that one is a "good person" is likely the single biggest mistake people make when building a self-image. The perception of oneself as a good person is nevertheless incorporated into almost every unexamined self-image. At a surface level, it is a good thing to incorporate altruism into your self-image, as it means you will experience more positive emotions from doing good deeds.

The problem is that self-images do more than affect when we experience positive emotions. Self-images also mitigate what evidence we are willing to internalize. If you place benevolence at the core of your self-image, you are unlikely to be able to realize when you are *not* acting with benevolence. Instead, you will begin to frame your thoughts and actions as "good." Almost no other characteristic of an internal self-image—outside of explicitly creating an evil internal self-model—will create a person more likely to commit "evil" acts than someone who is certain they are good.

A Protector of the Weak

A role as the protector of the weak is a remarkably common self-image type in which someone views themselves as a magnanimous protector of the weak and oppressed. On its surface, this sounds like a fantastic self-image. Seeing yourself as a protector of the weak allows you to feel positive emotions from helping those in need. Unfortunately, as with the self-image of a good person, the perception filter this self-perception creates is not worth the benefit.

A person who sees themselves as a protector of the weak will create a perception filter that does not allow them to internalize that whatever group they have come to see as weak may be in the wrong. What's more, an individual with this self-image is typically not able to perceive evidence that they may have been incorrect in their initial assertion as to which party was weak.

If reading the previous sentence gave you a flash of anger, it is likely that you have incorporated this into your self-image. You may be thinking: "obviously, everyone thinking clearly knows which party is weak and oppressed." However, whatever position you have taken regarding an obvious victim, it is likely you know of a group with the exact opposite perspective whose views you dismiss as evil, stupid, selfish, fringe, and maybe a little subhuman just as they dismiss yours.

There is no greater defense to justify bullying, thought policing, dehumanization, and terrorism than believing oneself to be "the protector of the weak." Almost every terrorist or censor in modern history was certain they were fighting on the side of the underdogs and protecting the weak.

Unsustainable Self-images

Watch out for self-images that involve something difficult to achieve or factors out of your control, such as the self-image of a professional athlete, model, or celebrity.

It is easy to achieve success early in life and incorporate that success into your self-image as your primary source of positive emotions—even if you logically understand the source of this success will not last for most of your life.

Even conceptualizing yourself as someone who does not tolerate failure is a dangerous move, as often our failures are out of our control. Avoid any self-image that revolves around transient factors that are outside of your control.

Self-Images that Rely Heavily on How others See You

It is normal to have some aspect of your self-image involve a desire to be respected or generally liked by those around you, but sometimes aspects of one's self-image that require external input can get out of hand. For example, some people have ingrained in their self-image that they must always be the smartest person in the room (note: This is not a part of their public persona, as they are not strategically portraying intelligence; instead, these people need to believe that they are the smartest people around in order to feel happy).

This self-image inevitably leads people to make counterproductive interactions in social contexts in order to maintain emotional stability.

This self-image can be remarkably problematic in the age of social media. To determine if this applies to you, ask yourself: "When I post something to social media, why am I making that post?" If you post to social media in a way that does not further your objective function, you probably have some aspect of this issue built into your mental model.

Normalizing Negative Behavior

It is easy to protect ourselves from our behavioral vices by saying that they are "just part of who we are." A person doing this may say, "I am just the jealous type," or "I have a fiery personality." Once you internalize statements like this you allow yourself to indulge in these emotions further reinforcing them, creating a cycle that normalizes the snowballing of negative emotional states. You only lack emotional control if you have convinced yourself you do.

Somebody Who Hates Being Rejected

No one likes being rejected. However, some people build into their self-image that rejection is devastating to them (rather than a minor inconvenience, which is arguably how a more well-balanced person would internalize such setbacks). Sure, rejection doesn't feel great, but it also doesn't really matter in the grand scheme of things whether or not someone else accepts you or likes you.

A fear of rejection typically emerges through a cycle of avoidance. In this cycle, an individual avoids situations in which rejection is a probable outcome. This reinforces the self-image of someone who is afraid of rejection and increases the individual's anxiety the next time that individual risks rejection—which will only strengthen the aversion.

Fortunately, avoidance cycles can be broken by simply creating a hard rule during your next flux period, decreeing that you never allow potential rejection to be a reason for not doing something. The important lesson to learn during this period is not that rejection comes less frequently than one expects, but rather that rejection really isn't so terrible.

Lower-Ranking Ideological Self-Images

Be wary of self-images that include a subordinate ideology—one that is not at the base of your ideological tree. Ideologies are hypotheses for maximizing an objective function. Hypotheses can be disproven. If one of your ideologies is disproven, it is in your best interest to discard it, which will be very difficult if you incorporate that ideology into your self-image. The only ideologies that are ever beneficial to incorporate into your self-image are those at the absolute base of it (i.e., religious ideologies).

For example, if you incorporate being a Republican into your self-image, you will no longer be able to internalize criticisms of the Republican platform.

In addition to blocking you from updating your position when better information comes along, self-identities shaped by lower-ranking ideologies make it difficult to promote those ideologies amongst others, as these identities prevent you from understanding their perspectives.

A person who identifies deeply with an ideology will have a filter on any information that runs contrary to their ideology, which makes it impossible understand the perspective of someone who doesn't hold that ideology, as both parties will be working with different perspectives and data sets. Even if you are nearly certain that the Republican party is the best way to achieve your objective function, you will still be better at spreading that ideology if you refrain from incorporating Republicanism into your identity.

Individuals who have incorporated an ideology into their self-image also run the risk of interpreting attacks on said ideology as attacks on themselves. If you can't help but get angry when someone criticizes an ideology you hold, you have probably built that ideology into your identity and should consider decoupling the two.

The danger of incorporating an ideology into your self-image increases in direct proportion to that ideology's distance from the base of your ideological tree. It is not nearly as damaging to incorporate an ideology like your religion into your self-image as it is to incorporate a political philosophy or affinity for a particular political candidate, thought leader, or religious leader.

All the disadvantages associated with incorporating an ideology into your image, such as the perception filter and a lack of ability to understand the reasoning of those with opposing views, will exist regardless of how low on your tree that ideology may sit. For this reason, it is still not great for an individual to incorporate their religious beliefs into their self-image, as this will make them much worse at convincing another to adopt it.

False Alarms

There are a few aspects of a self-image that one may initially internalize as being negative and worth changing which are actually benign or even beneficial.

Group Association

It is common for individuals to associate their identities with an external group. When the group is successful, the individual gets a psychological reward. When the group fails, the individual feels as if they themselves have failed. This can happen with groups ranging from sports teams to companies and nations. There is some thought in pop psychology that this is not healthy, but there is no concrete empirical evidence to back this up.

Still, it is worth considering whether this sort of identification is beneficial to your objective function. You should be aware of how group identities can affect your worldview. For example, an individual who strongly identifies with something external like a sports team often has "successes" and "failures" in life that are entirely outside of their control. To deal with this fact, individuals will often begin to adopt ideologies that give them a semblance of control over uncontrollable events, such as superstitions (e.g., "If I wear my lucky shirt during tonight's game, my team will win").

It is also important to be cautious about associating one's identity with a politician or political party. Demagogues are born when a large population sees themselves as being on the team of a candidate and ceases to critically question the candidate's actions. Supporters who incorporate a political leader into their identities will see doubt in this leader as a sign of cognitive dissonance and suppress it, which will ultimately contribute to fanaticism and prevent people from withdrawing support from politicians who begin to behave in dangerous ways.

Combined Identities

One self-image that is often derided as unhealthy or dangerous—but is actually very effective—is the "combined identity." Combined identities involve two (or, in very rare cases, several) people who conceptualize themselves as different avatars of a single entity rather than distinct individuals. We would go so far as to argue that for a married couple, a combined identity is ideal for almost any objective function (so long as the couple holds the same objective function). Once a combined identity is established, its constituent parts become more resistant to outside influence than stand-alone self-identities.

All that said, combined identities are dangerous when contrasted with other identities as there is the possibility that the identity is (1) unreciprocated and unsolicited (as with a stalker or codependent partner), (2) unreciprocated and downright predatory (as with an abusive spouse or cult leader), or (3) was formed under unstable circumstances (such as in high school). In all these cases, combined self-identities can cause significant harm.

Avoid Allowing Your Self-Image-Powered Autopilot to Make Major Decisions

This is one of the most important takeaways from this guide.

Most people live their lives almost completely on autopilot. If you do not make a concerted effort to think critically, your default self-image-powered autopilot will dictate not only your emotional reactions and the information you internalize, but also your major life decisions.

To better understand what this looks like, let us consider James. James gets an email from a friend requesting he join their trip to climb Kilimanjaro. If James determines his response while on autopilot, he will subconsciously ask himself: "Am I the type of person who would say yes when asked by a friend to climb Kilimanjaro?"

Assuming James sees himself as an erudite, well-traveled, adventurous, reliable friend, his autopilot will almost certainly lead him to say, "Yes!"

Were James to instead act pragmatically and submit this question to his higher cognitive functions, testing it against his objective function and ideological tree, his thought process would look quite different. He would think: "What will I/the world gain if I climb Kilimanjaro? What is lost if I climb Kilimanjaro? Can I logically justify the money and time I will spend on this trip? How many children could live a year on the money I am going to spend on this indulgence? Can I justify the tradeoff? Does climbing this mountain contribute to my objective function? Will spending days climbing up an arduous trail even make me happy?"

Being cognizant that we all default to the autopilot method for making decisions can substantially improve our lives by helping us (1) shake ourselves into a moment of lucidity when we realize we are about to make a major decision and (2) better model how those around us will likely react at decision points in their lives. By understanding how other people see themselves, we can predict their actions and reactions with a high degree of certainty.

How to Change

Earlier in this chapter, we discussed how to change our self-image by entering a period of flux. That said, self-images aren't the only aspects of our behavior we may seek to change, and periods of flux aren't the only way to change a self-image. Here we will review several systematized methods for realizing—and then securing—the change we want in ourselves and ensuring that our improvements stick.

Costly Thresholds

The start of almost any journey of real self-change should involve taking a step over a "costly threshold." A costly threshold is something of real and substantial cost to you that is symbolic of the change in yourself you wish to make. This cost doesn't need to be monetary, but instead can be a social cost or giving up something important to your identity/habits. Be sure the costly threshold you decide to cross is giving something up that it is not something easy to re-acquire, such as alcohol or TV—it must be permanently lost once given up, like a friend network, job, significant other, or money.

Costly thresholds help us clearly signal to ourselves that we have made a real change in our lives. They create cognitive dissonance when we fail to follow-through with the change tied to that threshold. We end up creating the thought pattern of, "Did I give up X for NOTHING!?" when we find ourselves tempted by old habits. Costly thresholds also help us see ourselves as different, new people, which is useful when committing to major character changes.

We strongly recommend anyone inspired to create a new public persona based on this guide to focus on a uniquely effective costly threshold: the outfit and persona change outlined in the next chapter. By changing the way you dress, you reinforce a change in your public and private persona. This is a uniquely effective costly threshold as it not only has the benefit of both monetary and social costs, but also forces you to intentionally contextualize yourself as the new "you" every time you suit up. Getting dressed as your "new and improved" self helps to keep you in character.

Confrontation Patterns

An easy way to ensure change in our behavior is to create extremely simple rules that we do not allow ourselves to break, ever. It is for this reason that abstinence is scientifically more effective than moderation from addictive substances. One of the most life-changing rules we can create for ourselves is a "confrontation pattern." This rule is specifically designed to help people who feel that they struggle with avoidance patterns.

An avoidance pattern begins when a person avoids something for what usually starts as a trivial reason (this process is also discussed in the "Reinforcement" section). For example, a person may have one negative social interaction at a party, then decide to not go to the next party based on a very slight impulse to not go. Not going to the next party reinforces a habit of not going to parties and the impulse to not to not go to future parties becomes stronger until eventually it snowballs and becomes crippling. This can happen with phobias around everything from dirty objects to flying and rejection (e.g., asking people on a date).

If you recognize that you have developed an avoidance pattern like this and view it as worth your time and effort to remove that pattern from you autopilot, create an opposite but equal set of rules you always follow to breaks it. For example, if you have developed a fear of going to social events, create a rule forcing you to attend any social event you are invited to on a night in which you don't have other plans and always follow that rule. This can quickly break impulses associated with avoidance patterns around social events.

Proselytizing

Surprisingly, one of the best ways to persuade yourself to maintain a change you have made in your life is to persuade someone else to make the same change. Having convinced another person to make a change in his or her life creates strong cognitive dissonance when you fail to make and maintain the same change in your life, especially when the person you helped points out your hypocrisy to you. In addition to creating cognitive dissonance when you are failing to live up to your values, proselytizing pragmatic values in general acts as a very real costly threshold in which the cost is the social capital you expend promoting a pragmatic outlook on life.

Say David convinces his wife Emily to adopt a pragmatic outlook on life and specifically to stop wallowing in self-hatred after making mistakes (pointing out that indulging in self-pity was not helping her achieve her goals). When Emily later calls David out for doing the exact same thing, she will cause him strong cognitive dissonance, which will make it very easy for him to stop indulging in self-pity.

Because proselytizing to a friend network can be particularly costly in terms of social capital, the Pragmatism Foundation will attempt to set up opportunities for individuals who want to proselytize about changes they want to make in themselves to strangers. For example, we may help you get a speaking gig at a local school where you give a presentation on not acting on anger. After giving a speech on a topic like this to children, most would feel quite silly allowing themselves, as grown adults, to succumb to anger and raise their voices at a loved one or friend.

Tokens

A token is a physical reminder you carry with you to remind you of some pledge you have made to yourself or some change you are trying to create in your character. Tokens are relatively low in terms of effectiveness but also low in terms of cost and can be a great addition to anything you are using to ensure personal change.

For a token to be effective, it should be acquired specifically in association with something you wish to change and be rare or unusual in some way. Examples may be a large old coin you keep in your pocket, or a hair clip you wear every day. While you can procure your own tokens, they can be more effective if given to you by another individual also trying to make the same change in their life you are. For example, if you have pledged to yourself to act more intentionally in accordance with applied pragmatic thought and meet someone through the Pragmatist Foundation who is taking the same journey, obtaining a small keepsake from them that you keep in your pocket every day can help remind you to focus on your goals.

Tokens are useful in that they are a physical reminder of something not to do. When you feel a tendency to do that thing you can reach into your pocket and hold them until that tendency dissipates. After a period of using tokens, you will no longer feel a desire to engage in the behavior they were reminding you to ignore. When this happens, the token can be ceremonially disposed of (throwing it in the ocean, burning it, etc.). Doing this creates a point in your mind from which which is difficult to regress without creating a huge amount of cognitive dissonance.

Association

One way to sustainably remove an unwanted habit is to associate it with something your core character despises (small mindedness, weakness, etc.). For example, if you want to stop drinking alcohol in excess, you may create an association between drinking in excess and weakness instead of the culture of your ancestors. It is easier to vanquish behaviors if you associate them with something for which you have visceral disgust.

Naltrexone

On the subject of strategies for overcoming biological addictions to substances like alcohol under control, let's talk about pharmacological interventions for dramatic self-reinvention. Naltrexone is an opioid antagonist and can be used to "delete" addictions fairly quickly through the Sinclair Method.

Essentially the Sinclair Method is entails taking a pill (Naltrexone) before engaging in whatever activity you are addicted to. In about 80% of the population, this causes the addiction to quickly fade because the neurological reward pathway that hijacks your brain to force you to do something that your logical mind opposes breaks. Naltrexone works great at tackling addictions to gaming, gambling, overeating, sex, and drinking, (the primary addiction against which Naltrexone is infective is nicotine due to different neurological paths being involved). It is uniquely great at handling addictions you don't want to totally shed.

While the use of Naltrexone for addiction treatment is common in some countries, it is fairly rare in the US, so if you want to get your hands on it in the USA one of the only strategies is to buy it illegally from shady Indian websites. That said, we are not recommending you do so, nor are we recommending the use of Naltrexone at all. You should consult your doctor and other trained professionals for help with addiction.

When Naltrexone *is* used in the US, it is (at least at the time of publication) commonly used incorrectly—as if it were an addiction suppressant to help with abstinence (which studies show is completely pointless). Even when you are not self-medicating, be sure to do your research! Naltrexone is just one of many examples how many medical professionals can fall behind on reading new research.

Social Pressures

One of the most effective but difficult-to-engineer mechanisms of maintaining desired change is sustained social pressure and group accountability. While it is easy to join a social group that will pressure you to be a certain way, it is much harder to join a social group that will pressure you to make the changes you want to make in yourself.

There are a number of somewhat independent mechanisms through which social pressures reinforce behavioral changes:

- **Conditioning:** Members of a group can push back when you do something out of line with your desired character. If you receive reliable and immediate negative or positive feedback in reaction to a specific behavior, you will be able to more easily correct said behavior.
- **Conformity:** As much as we hate it, we have an innate desire to "fit in with a group," so we might as well leverage this evolved tendency to our advantage. Part of fitting in with a group involves adapting to that group's normative culture. By creating groups with a beneficial normative culture and being clear that one of the group's core purposes is to provide beneficial normative culture, we can easily improve ourselves.
- **Group identity:** When we believe we "fit in with a group," we begin to adopt that group into our self-identities. This is an easy way to change the how we perceive ourselves.
- **Accountability:** When we know someone else is going to say or think, "You said you would do x but didn't follow-through," we are much more likely to follow-through than we would if we were only accountable to ourselves (it is easier to make sure you don't skip your morning jog when you are doing it with someone else).

Utilizing group influence to solidify the change we want in ourselves does not require large groups. Even a single additional person who helps you actualize the change you want in yourself can have an enormous impact. However, this impact will not be realized to its full potential unless you interact with said person in an intentional way.

One effective way to build this intentionality is for you and this person to adopt a daily routine such as a strategy walk or daily phone call in which you discuss your life strategy and how you are striving to achieve it daily. Not only does this create accountability but talking something through with another person allows you to access different thought pathways than those you access when writing or thinking by yourself (slightly different parts of your brain process spoken information when contrasted with written information, to tackle a topic with 100% of your potential you will need to both talk and write about it).

Without a social group, friend, or romantic partner who is willing to reinforce the change you want to see in yourself (or worse still, friends or partners who actively fight for the status quo), you will find improvement to be extremely difficult, if not impossible.

Thought Experiments

Most of the mechanisms for behavior change we discuss focus on changing the way you react to various stimuli. However, through changing the way you view situations in a systematic way you can systematically alter the stimuli, in turn changing behavior.

You may, for example, create a habit of believing that you will only have sustained free will for about the next five minutes and will only regain it occasionally. This is easy to believe because, as we have regularly discussed in this guide, your autopilot-impulse-driven behavior almost always overwhelms your lucid mind. In a very real way, you will not have free will for the majority of the future of your life.

Let's explore how this perspective change might play out in a few scenarios:

(1)
- **Impulse**: "I'll have an hour to do this project tomorrow, so I don't need to do it now."
- **Perspective shift**: "Do I expect that during that hour I have available tomorrow I'll actually do this project? What does my past behavior imply about whether I will actually do it?"
- **Result**: "Since I don't actually expect I'll spend that hour tomorrow doing the project, I'd better do it now."

(2)
- **Impulse**: "Once I'm back from vacation I'll start going to the gym every day"

- **Perspective shift**: "Based on what I know about myself, will I actually start going to the gym daily when I'm back from vacation? If I had to bet money on it, which side would I bet on?"
- **Result**: "Since I probably won't start going to the gym daily when I'm back from vacation as things currently stand, I'd better use the next 5 minutes to begin tweaking the situation to increase my odds of success, such as by picking the gym I'll go to, and asking a friend that lives nearby if he wants to go to the gym with me regularly."

(3)
- **Impulse**: "I don't need to make this decision about where to invest my money now; I can make it at any time."
- **Perspective shift**: "If I don't make this investment decision now, when do I predict I will actually make it? Will it be later this week, or more realistically, months from now?"
- **Result**: "Since this investment decision will never feel urgent, I know I'll probably by default put off making it for a long time, but since I don't have time to make the decision thoroughly right now, I should set aside 3 hours on Saturday to do it, which I can block off in my calendar right now."

(4)
- **Impulse**: "I'll choose not to eat those delicious cookies if I leave them on the kitchen table."
- **Perspective shift**: "Even if I successfully avoid eating the cookies on the table a few of the

times that I pass them, do I expect that I will avoid them every time? Or will eventually give in and eat them?"

- **Result**: "Since I am in control of the decision right now, I should put the cookies into a jar that is out of sight, so that I won't be tempted over and over again every time I pass the table."

This perspective shift is powerful for two reasons. The first is that is forces you to take ownership of your current behavior by jarring you into a state of lucidity. Secondly, it forces you to recognize that you can predict your most likely future behavior from your past behavior. For example, if you almost always drink more than you want to when you go out with your friend Don, you'll almost certainly do it next time too, unless something about you or that situation is significantly different next time around.

More generally, if you almost always do action A1 in situation S1, why would you assume you'll now instead do a different action—A2—in the same situation? The fact that you can "choose" to do A2 instead of A1 is not convincing because last time, and the time before that, you could have chosen A2 instead—but you didn't; you chose A1.

Whatever previously drove you to action A1 will likely cause drive you to A1 again. If you want to do A2 instead of A1, then you should do what you can right now (while you have awareness and control over the next 5 minutes) to change the future situation from S1 to S2, where S2 is a new situation that pushes the balance towards your choosing action A2 instead of A1. It could be that the change from S1 to S2 is a change you make in the surrounding environment (e.g., moving the cookies), or it could be a change in yourself (e.g., reminding yourself regularly about why you care about going to the gym), but whatever it is, it had better be a change. Otherwise, you're stuck doing A1.[8]

But it's Not That Simple

As much as we want a simple explanation for errant emotional states and human behavior, the nuances of this interaction are quite complex. Every human is ultimately a combination of their genetics, their life experiences, and who they choose to be. You have some control over how much each of those things makes up who you are, but you do not have the power to free yourself from one entirely.

What we have tried to focus on in this guide are aspects of human interaction over which we have the capacity to exercise control.

That said, there are factors that influence our behavior that are *outside* our control, and it is

[8] This scenario was authored in part by Spencer Greenberg founder of ClearerThinking.org.

worthwhile for us to be aware of them. These external influencers fall into five broad categories: genetic influencers, traumatic life events, addictions, priming influencers, and logical fallacies and biases.

Genetic Influencers

It is common knowledge that certain aspects of our personality are inherited. It is not unusual to hear someone state, "he has his father's hot temper," and not think twice about the implications, specifically that he either inherited a hot temper from his father in his genes or that he inherited the temper through how he was raised. Twin studies are studies in which scientists look for similarities more often shared by identical twins than by fraternal twins, allowing them to identify aspects of a person's character that are linked to genetics and not just how a person was raised. Such studies have provided a perpetually growing body of evidence that, yes, some portions of our personality are influenced by our genes.

Sometimes these genetic predispositions are as simple as an increased susceptibility to addiction while at other times they are significantly more nuanced, as is the case with mood disorders like bipolar and depression. There is copious evidence that such disorders are heavily reliant on our genetics. In the case of bipolar disorder, if one identical twin has it, there is a 60% probability that the other will have it as well.

There is even evidence that our genetic predispositions may extend beyond our personalities and into our ideologies. The nascent field of genopolitics specifically studies how our genes and brain morphology impact our political alignment. For example, one study published by Dr. Schreiber in 2013 indicates he could predict an individual's political affiliation with 82.9% accuracy by how their brain structures reacted during a gambling task. Despite a few flashy results like Dr. Schreiber's, the field is still in its nascency and may not carry as much weight as popular science magazines would have you believe.

Regardless of how new fields like genopolitics shake out, few in the scientific community would argue our genetics play no role in our cognition. Keep in mind that it is widely accepted that certain psychological conditions are, at their core, genetic/physiological in nature and that while the advice in this guide may help a psychologically healthy person achieve their goals, it isn't going to be effective at altering a physiological abnormality.

Traumatic Life Events

Occasionally a person may experience an event so traumatic it alters the way his or her brain works. People who suffer from extreme PTSD will have their hippocampus shrink significantly in size. The reactions that result from this sort of atrophying of a brain structure are not something that an altered image of your identity can overcome. Only specialized therapy can help. That said, such events are exceedingly rare.

Addictions

It should go without saying that addictions will influence your behavior and are to some extent beyond the control of your self-image (though not entirely). Addictions occur when the normal reward pathways in our brains that evolved to get us to act in beneficial ways become hijacked and begin to work in ways that harm us.

These hijacking factors can be obvious culprits like chemicals that directly act on our reward pathways (cocaine), overindulgence in stimuli that activate base reward pathways (food and exercise), and even indulgence in activities that simulate genuine accomplishment, thereby activating our brains' reward pathways (video games and gambling). It is worth noting that the level of one of these activities one must indulge in before addiction takes hold is heavily influenced by an individual's genetics.

Addiction exists within your brain's normal pathways. Your addiction isn't a small voice in your head nagging you to partake in an action that "the real you" knows is wrong. Your addiction has access to 100% of the mental processing capacity the rest of "you" does and will utilize that power to win any struggle against the "real you." Addiction being the result of disruption in your brain's intended pathways is why pharmacological intervention like Naltrexone enjoy success in combating addictions where logic alone fails.

Because the addicted version of yourself will always control your autopilot, the only way out of an addiction outside of a pharmacological intervention involves entering a period of flux and referencing your objective function to create an altered identity more capable of rejecting temptation (this is why AA forces its members to believe in a higher power, as it is the only objective function its creators could conceive of as being concrete and simple enough to counteract the autopilot controlling forces of addiction).

Finally, it is worth noting that, contrary to what one may assume, studies have repeatedly shown abstinence from whatever you are addicted to is much easier than moderation. When you think about this, it makes sense. Consider someone addicted to alcohol feeling an impulse to have a beer: the person can either go through the fairly simple mental processes of saying "I don't drink alcohol" to shut off the impulse or the more complex process of "How many beers have I had to-day? Was that too many?" The complexity of the latter process makes it less effective at combating the impulse to drink.

Priming Influencers

Simply put, priming takes place when exposure to one stimulus influences our response to another stimulus. For example, you will be able to recognize the word "nurse" faster after the word "doctor" than after the word "bread" because the neural pathways associated with medical professions has been primed and has an easier time activating.

Think of your brain as requiring a certain level of stimulation to pursue certain thoughts (e.g., there is a certain level of nurse related paraphernalia or letters in the word n***e you need to see before you think the word "nurse"). Similar but ultimately non-pertinent stimulation can lower this threshold dramatically (e.g., if you had heard the word "doctor" recently, you would think the word nurse at a lower level of "nurse" related input).

This lowering of thresholds isn't limited to simple thoughts; it can also include behavior patterns—even those we typically think of as "moral" and "social." Essentially, environmental stimuli priming us can cause us to act like different people. For example, people can be influenced to cheat less by being reminded of the Ten Commandments (even if they are not religious), signing a pledge to be honest, or even by viewing a pair of human eyes painted on a box (which gives the impression one is being watched and held accountable).

The easiest way to protect ourselves against the influences of priming is to mentally divide our internal model of ourselves into an "outer model" and a "core model." The more complex outer model is the part of us that directly influences our behavior and is susceptible to priming effects, while the inner model is the reference sheet we use to maintain the fidelity of the outer model as it morphs over time.

This morphing of our outer mental model over time is not a sign of personal failure and part of normal human life—unless, of course, we allow our entire self-image to be the product of priming and never self-correct when we feel ourselves drifting.

Logical Fallacies and Biases

Logical fallacies and biases are very much like optical illusions but in the way our brain processes information. In an optical illusion, we perceive the world incorrectly because our brain is taking a shortcut that usually works, but in rare instances causes us to misperceive reality (like how we perceive the spaces in between the squares in the image below changing from white to black due to lateral inhibition in neural pathways).

In the same fashion, shortcuts our brains use to effectively process the massive amounts of information we take in daily can sometimes lead us to perceive arguments as rational that are not or pursue behaviors that don't correlate with our self-image.

For example, we will perceive an idea that is popular as being more correct than an idea that is unpopular—even though we logically know that the popularity of an idea is not proof of its validity. We do this because most of the time, ideas that are popular have been vetted by other people and thus we do not need to personally expend as much mental energy validating them.

Fallacies and biases present a twofold challenge to a pragmatic outlook on life. First, studies have shown that even if we are aware of a bias, we are still susceptible to it. Worse, even if we succeed in admitting that we arrived at a conclusion due to an illogical bias, studies show we do not value that conclusion less. Even though we know the above picture is an optical illusion, we still see it as moving. So it goes with biased conclusions.

The second, and perhaps more damaging effect of biases and fallacies is that extensive knowledge about them does more to obfuscate our perception of reality than clarify it. Because knowledge of biases does nothing (or very little) to protect us from them, individuals with extensive knowledge of biases are more likely to use said knowledge to protect themselves from views that contradict their own rather than challenge their current worldviews. We will dismiss the ideas of others as being the result of a bias without truly processing those new ideas, but not use the same knowledge of biases to question our own ideas. (If you are someone who takes pride in your knowledge of fallacies and biases, honestly ask yourself if you have ever changed your own view of the world based on that knowledge.)

For this reason, while knowledge of biases and fallacies may help you win a debate, it will not help you improve yourself. The only two questions worth asking yourself to overcome a bias are: "Why am I doing this?" and "Why do I think this?" If you can train yourself to answer those questions honestly, the effect biases will have on you will be mitigated more than a lifetime spent researching logical fallacies and biases ever could.

Brain States Follow Physiological States

Sometimes our brains react emotionally to stimuli in very strange ways. It is common to hear things like: "Forcing yourself to smile makes you happier" and assume that you are hearing a pop-psychology myth. This is not the case. In fact, studies have even shown that Botox injections that paralyze the muscles in someone's face and prevent them from frowning will make them happier while removing laugh lines with cosmetic surgery will make someone more depressed.

The findings associated with smiling are not unique. There is a virtual mountain of studies showing that facial expressions, the way you move, physical actions, and the position of your body can all affect your mental state. Here a just a few examples:

- Striking a "power pose" will make you more confident and increase your testosterone levels while decreasing your cortisol levels
- Sitting with good posture will make you happier
- Nodding while being told something will make you more likely to believe it
- If you hug yourself, you can reduce the perception of pain
- If you sit up straight, you are more likely to remember positive memories
- Striking a constricted pose (keeping your limbs close to your body and occupying minimal space) will make you less comfortable making risky bets
- A slow slumped walk will decrease perceived energy levels while skipping will make you feel more energetic

---

Note: There have been recent studies challenging the facial feedback hypothesis as well as others that challenge the somatic marker hypothesis. This is the first case in this book where the two authors primary standard of evidence conflicts with Simone's being scientific method and Malcolm's being expert consensus within the scientific community. Simone believes that the current body of research no longer supports these theories while Malcolm believes it is not worth throwing them out until expert consensus has turned against them. We have chosen to leave this section as is but post this disclaimer as an example of how recognizing you are working off of a different standard of evidence than someone else can lead to a more productive discussion about the validity of an ideology.

Step 4: Define Your Public Character

Your public character is the person you present to other people. This character should be intentionally created to maximize your ability to achieve your objective function. You initially may not feel comfortable with the idea that your internal self-image and public character are different, assuming that your external character should always be the same as your internal character. At the very least, you may question why one should put effort into developing a separate external character.

In this chapter, we will review why it is necessary to create a separate external character and outline how to create an effective character for achieving your desired goals.

Why Have Differing Public and Internal Characters?

There are three core reasons to not use your internal character as your external character.

1) Your Public and Internal Characters are Not the Same Type of Thing

Your internal character is primarily used as a cheat sheet for your brain. Your internal self-image helps you decide how to react emotionally to stimuli and what information to dismiss without careful analysis. In contrast, your public character is what other people use to categorize you within their heads and determine what place you should have in their lives.

Asking why you cannot just use your internal character as your public character is like asking why Microsoft doesn't just write word processing application code on the box in which Microsoft Word is sold. While the code *is* Microsoft Word, it is not helpful to others to see the code when deciding how to use Microsoft Word in their lives. When selecting word processing software, people prefer to see pictures of word document editing interfaces and their features, which better communicate the way *they* interface with Microsoft Word.

2) Most People Lack Time the Understand Your Inner Character

It is narcissistic to assume people will (and should) invest the immense time and mental processing power needed to understand the inner you. You are an intricate, nuanced person. It would take someone years to comprehend you in all your beautiful complexity and yet the vast majority of people you will ever meet in your life will expend less than an hour of concerted focus getting to know and understand you. By insisting on displaying the "real you" in public, you are essentially demanding that people make an immense investment of time, thought, and emotion to understand you.

If we use the Microsoft Word analogy, this would be like a Microsoft employee arguing that if people "really cared about the product" they would take the time to read the code and understand it, when all the customer really cares about is how that product relates to them and what role it will serve in their lives, which is what the product's box art and advertisements convey.

If you present a well-crafted public persona (rather than your inner model of self), rest assured that some people will still come to know the "real you." It is reasonable to expect people like your spouse and closest friends to get to know your more nuanced inner self. Having a nicely packaged public persona does not prevent these people from getting to know the "real you." In fact, a well-constructed public persona may expand the audience of people who take the time to get to know the real you by enticing *more* people to want to know you better.

3) Internal Self-images Come Across as Forgettable and Bland in Public

Trying to publicly present your inner model of self will make you come across as bland and forgettable. When you attempt to portray the inner "you" in public, all people will be able to process in the five minutes (and that's being very generous) they spend thinking about you will not appear very different from anyone else trying to portray their inner selves (as opposed to a specially crafted public persona). Most normal, well-adjusted people in any given culture trying to show their "real selves" look 80% identical to everyone else trying to portray their real selves and thereby come off as bland.

Imagine that Microsoft Word and its competitors printed the source code for their respective word processing programs on their boxes. From the consumer's perspective, they would all look about the same. Even if someone did take the time to try to understand the code, the boxes would *still* end up looking indistinguishable, as huge swaths of each program are likely to be quite similar. In much the same way, two people who live in the same culture will almost certainly have 80%+ overlap in terms of who they "really are."

If instead of just publishing the source code on the box, software developers decided to publish a feature list, there would *still* be almost no differentiation between the various word processing software options—there would likely be at least 70%+ feature overlap (spell check, fonts, margins, etc.). This is the same with people. Even if you just try to give strangers a more easily digestible version of who you are, you will come off as very similar to anyone else who exists within your cultural context (e.g., you are a nice, clever, funny, loving person who is loyal to your friends and hardworking, but who likes to kick back and relax every now and then).

As with box art advertising word processing software, you need to focus on what is different about you. In the same way it would not make sense for Microsoft Word marketers to focus on spell check in advertisements and on box art (unless it had the best spell check feature in its class as reviewed by an independent study), it would not make sense for you to advertise how funny you think you are unless it is widely accepted that you are uniquely funny (e.g., you are a professional comedian).

However, this "box art" analogy only goes so far. While it does effectively illustrate that:

1. The purpose of your public personality is to help people contextualize what place you have in their lives,
2. That the vast majority of "the real you" will overlap with others in your peer group, and
3. The way most people will distinguish you from others is by specifically highlighting the ways you *differ* from others, and these characteristics may be far from what you would consider to be your core personality traits.

The analogy does not appreciate the unique manner in which our brain processes individuals.

In everything from facial processing to speech, the way our brains process social interaction is vastly different from how we process generic stimuli, such as vision of a grassy field or the sound of traffic. **Our brains use a series of ingrained pathways to take the enormously complex information about someone—collected over just few moments of exposure—and create a simple, realistically storable, mental model of who that person is.** By appreciating how this is done, we can create public versions of ourselves that are easier for people to interact with.

But I'm a Social Chameleon!

At this point you may be thinking: "Yes, I agree with you that my external character shouldn't be the same as my internal character, but that doesn't mean I need to expend mental effort creating one. I naturally and effortlessly adopt different external characters in different social groups and never have trouble blending in. I am a social chameleon!"

This is the equivalent of saying, "I am capable of coming off as generic in any context and am content with being forgettable." Effortlessly adapting to be invisible in different social contexts is a skill with which every socially competent human is born. People who do not exercise this ability are not doing so because of a lack of ability to fit in but because for whatever reason they want to leave an impact on people (assuming they have a base level of social competence). Sometimes the reason someone wants to leave an impact is puerile and self-masturbatory; other times a person desires to leave an impact to achieve a specific objective. Attempting to make the desired impact is difficult, risky, and something that even the most charismatic and tactful individual will fail at occasionally, which translates to having to deal with a chance of rejection every time you attempt it. To protect their self-images, many individuals who fear this rejection contextualize their genericness as a special skill—that of the "social chameleon."

As much as Western society denigrates the idea of being generic and forgettable, it isn't intrinsically a bad thing. In fact, being generic and forgettable could be the best path towards your objective function. For example, if you are just trying to maximize positive emotional states or believe the best way to impact the world is through operating invisibly, then the rest of this chapter will not apply much to you. However, it is important that you understand the logical underpinnings of the path you are intentionally taking and have it not be a path you chose by default out of a fear of rejection.

On the other hand, if you want to impact the world in a manner that leaves you personally remembered/recognized for your work, or should you wish to influence a large number of people through the avatar of your own person (e.g., if you want to be "classically successful"), then this strategy is patently ineffective. Obviously, it is still possible to be generic and accidentally fall into success put it certainly doesn't help your chances.

(Should you decide to skip the rest of the book, please leave us a review if you enjoyed what you've read. Positive reviews dramatically lower the cost of advertising the book. As all our profits go to nonprofit efforts like our school, every dollar not spent on advertising is one spent more directly helping people.)

Creating an Easily Digestible Public Identity

People are always the main characters of their own lives. To every single person who knows you and interacts with you, you are a side character, a supporting character. When you are creating your public identity, don't try to create the best protagonist you can, you are attempting to create the best supporting character you can.

Protagonists and supporting characters are written very differently for a good reason. For example, the most common protagonist type is the Mary Sue, but a Mary Sue type character in any role but the lead becomes the type of character that stands in the crowd and is played by an unpaid extra. Think about all of your favorite side characters from movies, books, and TV shows. Almost all of them will be bold, simple archetypes. This is because our brains hate to have nuanced processing foisted upon them. Our brains prefer that side characters be easy to categorize archetypes.

When "shopping" for whatever public persona you choose to adopt, sites like TVTropes.org are great places to look for inspiration. Keep in mind that, while there is no harm in borrowing the trope of a popular character type from media, you will be able to grab more mental space from others if you build the trope of a character that is not yet popularly depicted, but a trope society collectively "wished existed."

Examples of these powerful tropes emerging can be seen in public figures like Sarah Palin, Anna Wintour, Donald Trump, and George Takei. They presented personas to the world that were simple and easy to understand that fit in with existing tropes, allowing them to resonate strongly with the public. In some cases, the tropes that real people present through their public personalities work their way into popular media going forward.

When we say society collectively "wished these tropes existed," we do not imply that society necessarily *likes* these characterizations of people. We simply mean such tropes fit snugly into our brains as bold, simple, and easy to understand. Consider a character like Professor Umbridge from the Harry Potter series. Few people "like" Professor Umbridge, nor do they "want" her to exist, but even if you had never encountered her character before, were you to meet her in person, you would feel a sense of satisfaction with how snugly her character fits into your brain. Moreover, you would remember that person for years after only a brief encounter.

Ultimately, not everyone creating a public persona needs to focus on ease of digestibility. As stated before, this method is only necessary to study for individuals who want to be memorable, become effective leaders, act as influencers in interpersonal groups, and/or operate on a public stage.

Outlining your Public Persona

The following steps will have utility to any individual, even those that prefer to go unnoticed:

1. Identify what, specifically, you want to achieve in life to maximize your objective function. For example, you may decide you want to be a successful businessperson, an editor at a major

newspaper, a famous preacher, or a senior engineer at a major tech firm.

2. Make a list of individuals who have achieved these roles in the past. For example, a young woman who decides she wants to be a successful businesswoman might identify the top 100 most powerful women in business (removing all the women that had gained their power through paths not available to her like celebrity fame, inheritance, or marriage).

3. Carefully analyze these individuals. Read profiles on them, review their educational and job histories on LinkedIn or Wikipedia, watch their interviews and speeches, and listen to recordings of their voices. Look for similarities in the way they dress, speak, move, and ascend to their current roles.

This process will reveal common features of individuals who are successful in your field. Focus on the features that differentiate these individuals from societal norms, as any features that are societal norms are likely unimportant and only apparent because they would appear in any subsection of the population. What you must specifically attempt to identify is which traits, mannerisms, and outfits are common among this group of people successful in your desired field but uncommon among the general population.

Making the Change

Unless you have taken the above steps in the past or have very low ambitions for your future, you will likely realize that your current public identity is far from optimal for achieving your goals in life. The normal response for a human brain being told it needs to put significant effort into something is to scramble for an excuse that will allow it to maintain inaction and the status quo.

You may be thinking "I need to wait a while before making a major change in my personality, wardrobe, and speech patterns." This is nothing but a tawdry justification for inaction and is not true. Will some people ask you: "Why the change?" Probably. Will some people tease you? Maybe. Will the change be a hassle? Yes. But these issues are not important when contrasted with the potential benefits.

There will be no convenient time to rework your character. If you do not start now, you may never transition into the type of person you need to be to achieve your goals in life (or at the very least, you will add unnecessary difficulty to achieving your goals).

Moreover, making a concerted change to your public image has benefits that extend beyond how other people perceive you. Specifically, your new outfit and public personality act as a constant signal to yourself that you have made a conscious decision to change and improve. Wardrobe and appearance changes hold unique utility as they are monetarily and socially costly to adopt, which makes them a "costly threshold." If you are unwilling to step over that threshold, it is unlikely any of the changes you have decided to make to yourself through the course of reading this guide will stick.

The Importance of Flaws

"He has all of the virtues I dislike and none of the vices I admire."
- Winston Churchill

The first step in executing on the public persona you envision for yourself is to check it for viability. Is this character believable?

We previously mentioned that strong public personas:

- Are clear, compelling, and easily digestible
- Depict a character trope that is not yet common, but the world would love to see

But to be believable, strong public personas must also contain flaws. The single biggest mistake individuals make when crafting a public persona is attempting to craft a "flawless persona" that displays all virtues and no obvious vices. It is difficult to emphasize just how disastrous these "flawless personas" are to the way people perceive you.

When someone is asked by someone else (or asks themselves), "What is wrong with X person?" they will *always* come up with an answer. When you attempt to create a "flawless persona," that answer will be random (because nobody is going to believe you are perfect). By creating an "intentionally flawed persona," you can choose what people determine is wrong with you. In addition to making your public persona believable, a chosen flaw yields immense advantages.

Imagine two individuals: Kenneth and Ichiro. Kenneth chose to make a "flawless" public persona and only highlight virtues, whereas Ichiro choses to display his arrogance as a clear and public vice.

Whenever someone asks what is wrong with Ichiro, people always say he is arrogant. When people ask what is wrong with Kenneth, they make up an answer. If we ask ten people what is wrong with Kenneth and Ichiro, we will be told up to ten different things that are wrong with Kenneth, whereas we will only hear about one thing that is wrong with Ichiro (his arrogance).

If the people who know Kenneth ask each other the same question, one may say, "Well, I think

Kenneth is corrupt" and the other may say, "Yeah, well I think Kenneth is hiding something about himself." Now, each of these two people have *more* ideas about what is wrong about Kenneth: that he is both corrupt and a liar, whereas they only think one thing is wrong with Ichiro. As the example with Kenneth and Ichiro demonstrates, the negative effects of "flawless personas" scale with the scale of the arena in which an individual is playing.

The issue is extremely apparent in political races. Strong and obvious flaws combined with a powerful character grant a politician and his or her supporters a remarkable ability to shrug off attacks. Any jab opponents make about this politician's chosen public flaws enable a supporter to say "Well, sure, I already knew that." Claims of vices unrelated to this politician's public vices are easy to shrug off. "That's ridiculous," supporters say. "I know what's wrong with him and that's not it."

You can see this dynamic play out amongst candidates like Bill Clinton, Sarah Palin, Ronald Reagan, and Donald Trump. Attacks against Donald Trump claiming he wasn't good at business gained almost no hold in the media—despite ample evidence suggesting the attacks held weight. This is because such claims ran contrary to Trump's easy-to-digest persona, which proudly features a collection of obvious flaws. When people are told Trump is bad at business they think, "I already know what is wrong with Trump and that isn't it."

We would go so far as to say most presidential elections can be predicted by looking for the candidate with the less vague flaws. A candidate with vague flaws will almost always lose to a candidate with pronounced character driving flaws.

Think carefully about the flaws you will choose to exhibit in public.

There are two types of flaws we recommend considering:

- **Flaws that you can't seem to shake no matter what you do.** There may be some issues you have that would be impractically difficult to suppress or impossible to overcome. Consider unashamedly wearing these flaws on your sleeve. Winston Churchill offers a spectacular example of this. As, Tyrion Lannister, the vice-happy dwarf from Game of Thrones who at one point quipped, "Once you've accepted your flaws, no one can use them against you."
- **Flaws that "seem" terrible but that don't disqualify you from achieving your goals.** Bill Clinton's serial philandering may seem extremely negative to his opponents, however, in reality, nobody really cares (except his wife) and while some may view the behavior as immoral, it does not suggest Clinton is a dangerous or incompetent president and might even telegraph to many that he is a classic, dominant "alpha male" an element

people like in leaders (obviously, the concept of an alpha male has long been challenged as a scientific concept but it still exists as a trope in our society). We would go so far as to say the only thing about his philandering that rubbed the public the wrong way was that it wasn't with attractive enough women, which is the exception proving the rule (it was not within Bill Clinton's public character to be the type of person who slept with women who weren't classically attractive and therefore people took genuine exception to it).

A Note on Attractiveness and Moral Outrage: As every one-star review for this book mentions the above point, it warrants elaboration (this was true at the time this section was added; now a few negative reviews argue the book is boring, which we can't argue against). We do not claim that the public's distinctly negative reaction to Bill Clinton's philandering is a good thing—it's just a fact. Humans react with more moral repulsion on average to people acting outside of the stereotypes they've attached to them. The affair that ultimately inspired the House of Representatives to issue Articles of Impeachment against Bill Clinton did not involve a woman who looked like the "type" of person with whom the public expected a president to cheat, which exacerbated the media's resulting moral outrage.

The public's reaction to Bill Clinton's affair stands in stark contrast to the lack of moral outrage associated with the affairs between John F Kennedy / Marilyn Monroe and Trump / Stormy Daniels (the second of which happened after this book was released, somewhat proving the point—the public was more concerned about the affair's coverup than the affair itself, while the inverse was true in Bill Clinton's case).

This dynamic is also at play in rape-related court cases, in which, sadly, it has been found that attractive rapists get shorter sentences and people who rape less attractive individuals are seen as more personally culpable. This reality is horrifying and morally wrong, but such doesn't change the fact that it's reality. Humans judge the morality of actions based on the perceived attractiveness of the victims, and humans punish people extra for behaving "out of character."

(Should you be willing to cast a vote in favor of accepting inconvenient truths over uncomfortable realities, please drop us a review on Amazon. Now back to the book.)

When choosing a flaw in this category, make sure it is a genuine, maligned flaw yielding real social costs (but doesn't affect your specific goals). You will almost certainly be tempted to choose a flaw that doesn't really have a social cost (e.g., being clumsy). Harmless flaws have zero purchase in people's mental models and are the same as having a "flawless personality."

Outline Your Final Public Persona Carefully

When crafting a public persona, it is useful to outline its various component parts. These include (but may not be limited to):

- Clothing and accessories
- Styling (haircut, hairstyle, grooming, makeup)
- Predilections (what you drink, eat, and broadcast as a hobby)
- Speech patterns (accent, vocabulary, volume level)
- Public mannerisms (posture, gestures, movement)
- Goals and achievements (optimal graduate school degrees to obtain, job titles to strive for, club memberships to obtain, etc.)

Once you have created a basic outline, re-evaluate what you have. Ask yourself:

- Does this depict a character that is simple, memorable, and easy to digest?
- Is this character significantly different from the general population?
- Is this character in line with my internal personality model?
- Is this character in line with my ideologies?

- Is this character the best possible tool to execute on my ideologies in a way that will maximize my objective function?

You will likely need to refine this character quite a bit before it is ready for implementation. We strongly recommend discussing your reasoning and conclusions with a close friend who understands your goals and the framework presented in this guide.

Intentionally Managing your Social Network

Finally, we will briefly explore how to examine your interactions with others on an individual basis.

Our society treats friendship as some form of immutable magic in our lives from which we can only benefit. This view can be proven demonstrably false and toxic with even the slightest investigation. We all know of people with friends who do nothing but hold them back, enable their bad habits, or emotionally tear them down. A concrete *reason* stands behind every friend you have, as maintaining friendships requires effort that must be justified.

All friendships have a cost in terms of time. Because of this, the number of friends we can have is finite and every new friend you decide to manage not only precludes the possibility of another friendship, but also saps time you could spend doing something else. A poorly matched friendship could be preventing you from finding a friend who is a better match.

Whatever your objective function may be, managing friendships intentionally will always be superior to allowing friendships to form and fade serendipitously. The first step in managing your friend network is to take stock of it.

How to Take Stock of Your Friend Network:

- Create a list of who your friends are. Note why these people are your friends, and estimate the number of hours you spend each month interacting with each.
- Identify individuals who are either low utility to you or you don't really "like" being friends with. Dial down your interaction with them while dialing up interaction with "better friends."
- Identify areas in which your friend network is weak (e.g., you do not have any friends who live close to you, you do not have any friends you can bounce business ideas off of, etc.). Focus time and energy on shoring up those areas of your friend network by meeting new people in a directed manner.

- Optional: Use a free CRM system like Streak to manage your friend network efficiently, keep track of recent conversations, and remind yourself when you haven't contacted a friend in a while.

Types of Friends

When sorting through your existing friend network, it is useful to understand why someone is your friend. By determining the reasons why your friends are your friends, you can more easily decide how much time/effort to allocate to each person. Remember that every friendship you choose to maintain either represents another friendship that you will never have or time/resources that could otherwise be directed towards other areas of your life.

There are four common types of friends:

- Utility Friends
- Convenience Friends
- Character-Reinforcing Friends
- Character-Inclusive Friends

Utility Friends

Utility friends are friends that have access to a limited exclusive resource you value (or may have access to such a resource in the future).

Relationships with utility friends are primarily driven by access or potential future access to an exclusive resource. This resource can range to anything from sex, knowledge about a certain topic, good life advice, social capital, money, business contacts, access to parties/venues/clubs, interesting ideas that challenge you intellectually, social status, etc. Many of the resources we seek through utility friendships are non-economic in nature and instead revolve around things like spirited debate, the ability to intellectually challenge you, or the ability to expose you to new ideas.

As emotionally healthy individuals reach middle age, utility friends typically comprise the majority of their friendships as it is difficult to maintain large friend networks and, with all else being equal, a friend that has something to offer you or who can improve you as an individual is always going to be preferable to one who cannot.

Convenience Friends

Convenience friends are friends that you associate with primarily because you naturally encounter them on a regular basis. Convenience friends include people ranging from classmates to colleagues, roommates, family members, neighbors, fellow hobbyists, or people who frequent your favorite bar.

Convenience friends are not people with whom you have any special connection other than the emotional connection humans inevitably develop between people living in close proximity (so long as they do not actively dislike them). This connection feels special to people—especially younger, less-experienced people—but it is a feeling that humans inevitably form with any group of "allies" who operate in close proximity for long periods of time.

When we are younger, convenience friends will make up the majority of our friendships. With age and relocation, the transient nature of these relationships becomes apparent and they decrease as a portion of our friend networks. Normal, emotionally stable adults regularly replace old convenience friend groups with new ones as life circumstances change (i.e., when they leave a job, while they may stay in touch with a few coworkers, those co-workers will largely be replaced as friends by your new coworkers).

The earlier in life we learn not to invest significant time in convenience friendships, the better off we are in the long run. Whenever you enter a new environment, try to meet as many individuals as possible and get to know them as well as possible.

Having met a large sample of potential friends, focus building relationships with the ones who yield some form of utility. This is not what you will do on autopilot; studies have repeatedly shown that the friends we invest the most time and emotions into are those that are serendipitously placed closest to us (such as individuals who happen to work on your floor at work or those who live next door).

Ideally, most of your friends—especially those to whom you devote significant time and resources—will be utility friends. Again, remember that every friendship you settle on takes the place of another friendship or project you will never get to explore as your time is inherently limited.

Character-Reinforcing Friends

Character-reinforcing friendships help us better align ourselves with our internal self-images. Examples of friends who fall into this category include:

- People you are still friends with only because you don't like to see yourself as someone who casts off old friends as your life moves on (e.g., convenience friends who no longer are convenient).

- People who you haven't cast off as friends because they don't have many other friends and you want to see yourself as nice.
- People you remain friends with to relive moments of some past part of your life you cling to or with whom you share a memory that is important to both of your identities.
- People you are friends with because of their minority status (e.g., a token gay/black/white/Asian/Latino/etc. friend that reinforces how magnanimous and unbiased you are).
- Someone you are friends with as your "zany" friend with a lot of character.
- Someone you are friends with because the kind of protagonist you see yourself to be needs that sort of supporting character (such as a dashing husband, a sibling struggling with addiction/mental illness only you can save, an admiring mentee, etc.) to make sense.

This type of friendship becomes increasingly common through high school/college and again in old age.

A character reinforcing friend is arguably the best type of friend to *be* to someone else because it requires the lowest time investment on your part. Conversely, a character-reinforcing friend is the worst type of friend to *have* as this friend type costs the most in terms of time investment to maintain (by definition, they are not convenient) and offers you nothing in return other than the positive emotions that come with character and self-image alignment.

Everyone will always have a small handful of friends who fall into this category; however, we strongly recommend limiting that number to five and dispersing those five character-reinforcing across life stages.

Character-Inclusive Friends

This is by far the rarest category of friendship and is composed of a friend that is actively part of your self-identity or public identity. People in this category interact with either the world as a whole or a certain subcategory of the world (such as their high school) as a single unit.

There are three core subgroups within this category:

- Romantic partners in which both of you present yourself to the world as a single entity. Note that many romantic partners do not fall into this category and, in those cases, are utility friends. For early life relationships, the utility friends model for a relationship is typically superior due to its lower complexity, however the character-inclusive model for a relationship becomes viable with extremely long-term romantic partners.

- Best friends are a type of character-inclusive friendship very common in younger life in which you and one or more individuals present yourselves to the rest of your school's social world as a single unit. This is often an effective strategy for having backup in otherwise difficult times in our lives. However, as soon as you leave high school, no matter how much these people felt like BFFs, these friendships will transform into either character reinforcing friends or will drop off your radar altogether because you will no longer be able to present yourself to the world as a single entity. Buying into the illusion that character-integrated best friends will always have a unified public image with you can encourage very unwise decisions (such as following a best friend to the same college when you got into a better one).
- Parents who incorporate their children into their self-images. Such individuals are common amongst parents who feel that their own lives have little value and thus find themselves unable to build a self-image that satisfies them without leaching off the life of another individual.

Ultimately, all friendships fall into one of these four categories, but a friendship can contain elements of multiple categories and evolve between categories (most utility friends start as convenience friends). Being aware of what type of friend you are to others and what types of friends others are to you can help you see through the distortion field of emotional attachment that can lead to poor decisions that are not optimal for your objective function.

Note: Since the original publication of the book my co-author, Simone, was diagnosed with autism. The view of friendship she created for this book was cited in her diagnosis. But here's the thing: I, Malcolm, am not autistic and I think an objective look at reality says she is correct. Apparently, not accepting society's delusions about the magic of friendship is a component of an autism diagnosis these days.

Simone's diagnosis may explain why she was interested enough in understanding how humans think and process emotions to spend years working with me to develop predictive models for their behavior, testing those hypotheses, and writing a series of books on the subject. I am lucky to have found someone like her. (Oh, and if you want to find a great partner, be sure to check out our next book, The Pragmatist's Guide to Relationships.)

Bonus Step: Choosing a Culture

In the years following this book's initial publication we have had a chance to speak with many readers. A common theme that arises in conversation is discomfort with the role culture plays in readers' lives, be it a parent's culture, a religious culture, an ancestral culture, or an adopted culture.

We define culture as an interlocking set of values and schema about the world that interact with superficial identifiers such as accents, mannerisms, and fashion. Culture can play an important role in how we conceptualize our place in the world.

The right culture can help you (and your family) internalize and strengthen certain elements of your identity. Cohesive cultures provide a series of cues reminding you about your objective function and ideologies. Culture can influence your autopilot behaviour, even when you are forced to operate in suboptimal conditions.

Think of culture as the costumes and props on a movie or theatrical set. These elements alone will not create a compelling performance, but they certainly help.

Culture enters people's lives through a variety of interweaving pathways. While religious and ethnic cultures dominate, cultures born from discrimination and temporary developmental stages also have significant sway, plus many choose to develop cultures of their own, intentionally establishing new traditions for themselves and their kin.

For a far more in-depth exploration of culture and religion, their effects on adherents, and important things to consider when reinforcing an existing culture or religion (or creating something new from whole cloth or a patchwork of different sources), check out The Pragmatist's Guide to Crafting Religion.

Culture and Religion

Religion relates to us in three distinct ways:

- As a source for defining an objective function
- As a source for building an ideological tree
- As a source of cultural predilections, traditions, and identity

It is possible to have 1 & 2 without 3 and vice versa. For example, a person may believe a religion while simultaneously believing that its culture and traditions corrupt that religion's prescribed objective function. This can be seen in the disgust with which some fundamentalist sects regard traditions like Santa Claus and the Easter Bunny. A truly pragmatic religious devotee will take inventory of their objective function and test it against traditional practices associated with their religion, discarding those which impede their ability to maximize their objective function. For example, they may ask, "Does celebrating Easter with my kids bring them closer to God?" and find the answer is no.

Conversely, many stop believing in their religion as a source of purpose or as an explanation for how the world operates while still drawing from it as a source of traditions and cultural identity. A prominent example of this is the "secular Jew," someone who maintains a Jewish identity and incorporates Jewish traditions into their lives while maintaining a functionally atheistic worldview.

We, Simone and Malcolm, fall in this category. While atheistic in both our objective functions and ideological trees, we are relatively strict Calvinists when it comes to culture. We even identify as "Secular Calvinists" over identities like "atheist." You could argue the entire *Pragmatist's Guide to Life* is so heavily influenced by a Secular Calvinist perspective that it is, at its core, just a prescription for how a Secular Calvinist should approach life.[9]

---

[9] The Calvinist tradition holds that it is for everyone to interpret the Bible themselves without outside influence and that a person cannot arrive at truth

If we believe that Calvinism does not present a compelling objective function or explanation of how the world works, why would we be attracted to its cultural mores?

Only recently did humans have sufficient information to rival theistic hypotheses when exploring the origins of life and the universe. In contrast, our cultural traditions are the product of hundreds of centuries of cultural evolution. Cultures contain insights that cannot easily be uncovered a priori. For example, almost every religion on earth has some sort of arbitrary self-denial ritual (Lent, Ramadan, the Sabbath, etc.). Many atheists viewed these traditions as pointless until about a decade ago. Now we know that inhibitory pathways in our brains need regular exercise to stay strong and if they are not regularly exercised through systematic and arbitrary self-denial, we may see virtues like mental control and grit erode while certain vices—such as anger and anxiety—snowball.

How much of what we inherit from our family comes from genes vs culture is up to debate. What is *not* debatable is that we *do* inherit traits from our

---

through someone's external guidance. *The Pragmatist's Guide to Life* presents a similar approach without assuming the supremacy of the Bible.

family. A family's religious culture can be fine-tuned over generations, helping members of each generation optimize as people. Our Calvinist tradition, for example, imparts an extreme distrust of excess: indulgences in positive or negative emotional states as well of financial luxuries. While we can't be sure of the method of action, adopting this mindset significantly improves our overlay states and efficiency.

We have anecdotally noticed a correlation between rejecting cohesive cultural identities/traditions and experiencing more frequent, intense negative overlay states (though, it is possible that being unhappy causes a person to question culture more aggressively).

We are not opposed to forging new ways of living—society is better for people who innovate new cultures because they move things forward. That said, cultural trailblazers often sacrifice their own happiness to run what are essentially "cultural experiments." The mad inventor would not be "mad" if he didn't occasionally end up holding a now-empty test tube with soot on his face and his eyebrows singed off. Because they are forging a new path, those who move the furthest from their traditions (either voluntarily or because society cut them off) may struggle more to find contentment and emotional stability in their lives.

Cultures Born from Discrimination

As we discuss in greater depth in *The Pragmatist's Guide to Sexuality,* discrimination can drive those who face public persecution to commune with each other in private. This can foster the development of new, underground cultures through a process called "cultural drift," which has produced many now-iconic, influential, and cohesive cultures complete with unique traditions, values, and mannerisms (think: LGBT culture).

While these cultures may have a place in your life if you fall within an associated discriminated group, they are not a mandate. It is OK to be part of a historically persecuted group and not feel personal affinity toward the culture that formed around it. We say this, as a feeling of disconnect between an element of one's identity and that attribute's associated culture can cause significant cognitive dissonance. You are not more or less "X" because you participate (or don't participate) in "X" culture.

Ethnic Cultures

While ethnic cultures might be seen as overlapping with cultures of groups facing discrimination, they stand on their own (Han culture, for example, may be marginalized in the USA, but not in China). A common crisis among those who live by ethnic cultures arises from the mismatch between the ethnic culture with which they grew up (internal to their family) and the "true, historic version" of this ethnic culture.

Cultures evolve to fit their context. A more historically accurate execution of cultural traditions may work better for you, but ultimately it is your choice. There is no such thing as the "correct" manifestation of a culture. This is especially important to acknowledge given how frequently people discover what they believed to be traditional cultural practices are, in actuality, artificial previsions of that culture that had been marketed to them through media.

Evanescent Teen Culture

Many teens experience an innate desire to reject their parents' culture while simultaneously feeling very attuned to the feelings and caprices of peers their age. This often drives adolescents to "shop" for new cultures, only to return to a modified version of their ancestral culture upon reaching adulthood and having kids of their own (unless they experience systematic discrimination, which shifts identification toward the culture of their persecuted group).

This cycle produces evanescent teen cultures—or cultures specifically marketed to teens. Consider goth, emo, or e-girl culture—each of which features distinctive accents, dress, values, mannerisms, literature, and traditions. Evanescent teen cultures are hardly novel—consider dandy/macaroni culture as an older example.

Adolescent cultures evolve much faster than mainstream or religious cultural traditions, typically die out after a few decades, and are not conducive to happy, successful lifestyles. Rather than optimize for traditional success, contentment, or flourishing, evanescent teen cultures typically emphasize personal agency and uniqueness (highly rewarded attributes among teens).

Cultural Representation & Extinction

On its surface the idea that not seeing one's culture represented in popular media would cause distress or some sort of developmental damage makes superficial sense. In actuality, it is largely irrelevant when contrasted with other forms of cultural erosion.

Much of the hand wringing around cultural representation comes from the belief that "white" culture is a unified cultural force that is winning and in opposition to other cultural forces. This is not true, "white" culture is only the predominant culture as reflected by our society because whites make up the majority of the population creating the illusion that the majority "vanilla" culture is white.

For example, we think of the "Western" trope or "rural ranch family" trope as being representative of "white culture" (think Apple Jack from My Little Pony) when in actuality these tropes are heavily Latin in influenced. This can be seen from their dress like "cowboy boots" and "cowboy hats" to their values like "tight family units that unconditionally love and support each other". Alternatively, the more "traditional" white American cultures have largely been erased or villainised.

Take my culture, Secular Calvinism, as an example. Calvinists where major forces in the creation of American Democracy, the abolition movement, the enlightenment, and some sources credit them almost entirely for modern capitalism, you could not get more "white" or "American" – yet I can think of almost no media that positively displays my culture, most displaying it as the antagonist of the story (Footloose as an example). In fact, I remember how surprised I was to see a positive depiction of it in media for the first time – it was something only possible in a non-western source (a rather vulgar anime called Goblin Slayer).

However, it is not surprising that a culture that views any form of non-mission directed emotional indulgence as inherently evil does not find itself represented in media. A culture that looks down on art, music, and fiction as the height of self-glorifying navel gazing is intrinsically not going to produce a large quantity of artists and be an antagonistic force in the lives of artists who grow up within it. Sometimes, cultural representation is as much the fault of the "culture" as to society.

As another example, "Quaker culture" despite being critical to American history and a huge factor in many children's life's (due to its prolific production of teachers and impact on the education system), produces almost no one who goes into media while Jewish culture, which makes up only a tiny precent of American's produces an astronomical number of writers and comedians. In the same breath American Black culture, despite blacks only making up about 20% of the American population, is the progenitor of almost all American music varieties (yes, even both Country music which evolved out of Blues and Southern Gospel and Rock music which evolved out of Gospel, Jump Blues, Jazz, Boogie Woogie, and RnB). Well over 60% of almost any song you hear in the radio is a product of American Black culture.

However, and this is the important thing, cultural representation does not equate to power, a sense of belonging, or, most importantly, stave off cultural extinction. Gay culture had an overrepresentation in American media production long before it was accepted and, while black culture is the source of almost all modern music, only the most delusional individual claims blacks are not still discriminated against to at least some extent.

In fact, media representation is largely irrelevant to a cultures health. Calvinist's despite being one of the most important cultures in the creation of our current society have largely disappeared as a cultural force – not because of their lack of media representation – but because the culture categorises sex as a vulgar emotional indulgence and that love for family is strictly conditional (family members most prove their worth through action) thus produces relatively small families which culturally quickly expel members who don't live up to the cultures exacting value system. In a similar vein another of the most important early American cultures, the Shakers, have almost entirely disappeared due to similar, though more extreme, views towards sex.

The Shaker culture replicated itself through being the biggest owner of orphanages in early America. As soon as publicly funded orphanages started to compete with the Shaker orphanages the culture lost its ability to replicate and died.

The larger point here being that cultural competition and evolution is far more complex than dominant cultures victimising non-dominant cultures through media.

Constructing Culture

What if you want to attempt to build your own family culture or modify an existing cultural schema?

Culture is best transmitted through traditions and media. For example, to develop a bespoke culture that reinforces our unique values and ideologies, we modified existing holidays and created a few of our own, focusing on rituals that appeal to kids (traditions often live or die based on how much kids like them—this is why Halloween thrives while Lent languishes). We also curated a selection of materials to either read to our kids or regularly watch together and discuss, each of which features its own lessons related to our family values and ideologies.

Culture is just another aspect of a well-rounded education. It is our job to provide a rich upbringing for our kids without getting too experimental and endangering their ability to thrive. (We might put together a book on this one day.)

We Sincerely Hope This Has Been Helpful

It is ironic that we have an education system in which nearly everyone memorizes Socrates' adage that "the unexamined life is not worth living," but almost no one is ever seriously encouraged to examine their life. There isn't even a place we can go or a group we can talk to about such topics that won't push their own dogmatic agenda on us.

It is absurd that we live in a society where I, Simone, was able to reach my twenties before someone—that is, Malcolm—prompted me to decide what I wanted to do with my life in a way that actually enabled me to think about to carefully think about what values and outcomes truly mattered to me instead of just blurting something generic like "helping people" in an effort to change the subject. It is equally remarkable that no one ever made it clear to me that I could pick who I wanted to be in life—that I had the power to choose to be anyone I wanted to be. This needs to change.

These are questions people should repeatedly encounter outside of the pedantic halls of academia. These are questions with which people should interact using their own, carefully-thought-through frameworks. To that end, the proceeds from this book series all go to The Pragmatist Foundation, the primary goal of which (at present) is to create a new, better, secondary school system: CollinsInstitute.org

While this guide was the first product of our foundation, we have since created a few additional bestselling (on Amazon/Kindle) books designed to tackle other issues that traditional academic systems have difficulty addressing without bias. These books include:

- The Pragmatist's Guide to Relationships Ruthlessly Optimized Strategies for Dating, Sex, and Marriage
- The Pragmatist's Guide to Sexuality
  What Turns People On, Why, and What That Tells Us About Our Species.
- The Pragmatist's Guide to Governance
  From high school cliques to boards, family offices, and nations: A guide to optimizing governance models
- The Pragmatist's Guide to Crafting Religion
  A playbook for sculpting cultures that overcome demographic collapse & facilitate long-term human flourishing

If you enjoyed *The Pragmatist's Guide to Life* and are looking for a partner, experiencing trouble in your relationships, or just interested in why "weird" things turn people on, these books may yield helpful insights and information that you are unlikely to find elsewhere.

If you ever want to help edit, write, or otherwise contribute toward this series (or our school), please reach out. Each one of these books was a collaborative effort involving about thirty people and every additional hand makes a difference. Please let us know if there are any topics you want us to cover that we have yet to address. We love hearing from readers at: hello@pragmatistfoundation.com

We hope reading this guide has been helpful and will continue to do everything in our power to improve its utility. Since we take no money from this effort, we are paid in positive reviews and the joy of seeing people interested in our cause. If you gleaned any value from this book, please write a review (we guarantee we will read every single review posted on Amazon). In the same vein, if you didn't like something in the book, please send us an email (we have made a number of fairly major changes based on such comments).

Our Objective Functions

In case you are curious: Our personal objective functions are to increase the efficacy of humanity's collective mental substrate—that is, to encourage as many minds as possible to be (1) open enough to new ideas so they can test them against existing ideas, and (2) logical enough to let the best ideas win. To do our part in creating a world in which the best ideas win, we see our first big challenge being the creation of a world in which people are willing to consider ideas that conflict with their existing worldviews in a serious and thoughtful manner and creating venues where such conversations can be had.

Made in the USA
Las Vegas, NV
22 April 2024

89013876R00174